In Honour of

SHAKESPEARE

In Honour of
SHAKESPEARE

THE HISTORY AND COLLECTIONS OF THE SHAKESPEARE BIRTHPLACE TRUST

by

LEVI FOX
Director of the Trust

PUBLISHED BY JARROLD AND SONS LIMITED, NORWICH
IN ASSOCIATION WITH
THE SHAKESPEARE BIRTHPLACE TRUST
STRATFORD-UPON-AVON
1972

Contents

THE SHAKESPEARE BIRTHPLACE TRUST

THE SHAKESPEARIAN PROPERTIES

THE BIRTHPLACE COLLECTIONS

ILLUSTRATIONS

SHAKSPEARE'S HOUSE,

AT STRATFORD-ON-AVON.

THE MOST UNIQUE RELIC AMONGST ENGLAND'S TREASURES

AND INDEED, THE

MOST INTERESTING MONUMENT OF THE POET'S FAME which this Country boasts.

MR. ROBINS

Feels highly flattered at having been selected by the Representatives of the late Mr. THOMAS COURT,

TO SUBMIT TO PUBLIC COMPETITION,

At the Auction Mart, London,

On THURSDAY, the 16th day of SEPTEMBER, 1847,

AT TWELVE O'CLOCK,

THE TRULY HEART-STIRRING RELIC OF A MOST GLORIOUS PERIOD,

AND OF

ENGLAND'S IMMORTAL BARD,

Which, by the course of events, and directions contained in the Will of the late Owner, must be offered to Public Sale; yet with every fervent hope that its appreciation by the Public will secure for it a safeguard and continuance at the Birth and Burial Place of the Poet,

The most honoured Monument of the Greatest Genius that ever lived.

To attempt to panegyrize this interesting and singular Property would be in vain, for (to quote the Poet's beautiful lines)—

> To gild refined gold, to paint the lily,
> To throw a perfume on the violet,
> To smooth the ice, or add another hue
> Unto the rainbow, or with taper light
> To seek the beauteous eye of Heaven to garnish,
> Is wasteful and ridiculous excess.

Mr. ROBINS, therefore, simply invites all who take an interest in this monumental relic (and who is there amongst us does not), to pay a visit to Stratford-on-Avon, in the full assurance that what they will see and feel, now that this remarkable Property may be possessed, will raise a spirit of competition hitherto unknown.

The SWAN and MAIDENHEAD, a thriving Public-house,

Which adjoins, with its Out-buildings, forms part of the Property, extending from Henley Street to the Guildpits,

The whole of which, be it remembered, is FREEHOLD.

THE BOOKS OF AUTOGRAPHS with numerous poetic inspirations, CURIOUS ANTIQUE FURNITURE, and SEVERAL INTERESTING RELICS, will be Sold at the same time.

Visitors may, as usual, inspect this singular domicile; and Printed Particulars, containing a Copy of the Family Pedigree, and much that will interest the reader, with Vignette Views, a Plan of the Property, and a Frontispiece in character with the period, may be had (at 2s. 6d.) Six Weeks prior, at the Swan and Maidenhead, Stratford-on-Avon; the Bedford Hotel, and Mr. ELSTON's Library, Leamington; Dee's Royal Hotel, Birmingham; of WALTER JESSOP, Esq., Solicitor, Cheltenham; at the Auction Mart; and at Mr. ROBINS' Offices, in Covent Garden, London.

Alfred Robins, Printer, 7, Southampton Street, Strand.

Beginnings

The Shakespeare Birthplace Trust came into existence in 1847 with the purchase of Shakespeare's Birthplace by public subscription for preservation as a national memorial. The announcement of the sale of 'Shakespeare's House' at Stratford-upon-Avon, described as 'the truly heart-stirring relic of a most glorious period, and of England's immortal bard . . . the most honoured monument of the greatest genius that ever lived', had aroused considerable national interest and concern, with the result that committees were set up in London and Stratford to raise funds to purchase the property. When the sale took place at the Auction Mart, London, on 16 September 1847, the sum of £3,000 secured the purchase of the property for preservation as a national memorial to the dramatist.

The immediate object of the purchase was to rescue the much neglected fabric of the house in Henley Street from disrepair and, as *The Times* said in its leading article, 'to secure it against being exposed at any future time to the chances of desecration, destruction or removal'. Visitors to the poet's birthplace had in fact for some time past been shamelessly exploited and public opinion now demanded that the property should in future be administered in a manner befitting the memory of the national poet.

The original idea was to place the property, once purchased, under the protection of the Government, but protracted negotiations with the Commissioners of Woods and Forests (predecessors of the Commissioners of Works and Public Buildings, later the Ministry of Works, which is now incorporated in the Department of the Environment) proved unsuccessful. Instead the Stratford Birthplace Committee took the initiative and, in spite of many difficulties, assumed responsibility for liquidating the debt incurred by the purchase and for raising further funds to make possible the repair of the property.

The anxieties and problems of these early years can be followed in detail in the minutes and annual reports of the Committee. In the absence of subsidy from public funds, the Trustees had to rely on subscriptions collected and on the income derived from the admission fees paid by those who wished to visit the Birthplace. They appointed a custodian, fixed the admission charge at one shilling, and generally ordered the arrangements for the day-to-day running of the property. An official Visitors' Book was instituted. In 1853–4 as many as 2,878 persons visited the Birthplace, and these included visitors from Holland, Turkey, the U.S.A. (as many as 461), Jamaica, Australia, Ceylon, Austria, Hong Kong, Denmark, Canada, Belgium, France, Norway, Newfoundland and Hungary.

Between 1857 and 1864 the Trustees undertook in stages a careful restoration of the fabric of the building; and the garden was laid out with 'Shakespeare's trees, plants and herbs'. But the Birthplace was not to be regarded merely as a preserved relic; it was to be used as a means of furthering knowledge and appreciation of the life, work and times of William Shakespeare. Hence the Trustees began to assemble the nucleus of the Birthplace museum and library.

Important early acquisitions were the collections of Robert Bell Wheler and Captain James Saunders. The Town Council showed its interest by placing the town records and other civic items in the Birthplace, and the Governors of the Grammar School by depositing a sixteenth-century desk (traditionally 'Shakespeare's desk') from the school. Slightly later, J. O. Halliwell-Phillipps and W. O. Hunt made considerable gifts of books, and in 1864 the Ely Palace portrait of Shakespeare and the old oak chair from the Falcon at Bidford (known as 'Shakespeare's chair') were presented. These were the beginnings of the Trust's present collections of books, original documents, pictures and museum items illustrative of the life and works of Shakespeare, and of the history of Stratford-upon-Avon and locality.

Early Growth

In consequence of the death of two members of the Committee in 1866, it was decided to convey the Birthplace property to the Corporation of Stratford-upon-Avon and to entrust its management to a Committee consisting of certain life trustees, together with *ex-officio* personages of the town and county. A deed of trust dated 4 July 1866 detailed the new arrangement, which lasted until 1891 when the Shakespeare Birthplace Trust Act formally incorporated the Trustees and Guardians of Shakespeare's Birthplace. The Act vested in the Trustees the Birthplace property, to be kept as 'a permanent and national memorial to William Shakespeare'; and also Shakespeare's New Place estate where the poet had lived in retirement and died, which had been purchased independently by public subscription as a national memorial in 1862, largely due to the enthusiasm of J. O. Halliwell-Phillipps. The Act contained express provisions for the maintenance of a library and museum in connection with Shakespeare's Birthplace and authorised the Trust to acquire any other properties 'which are of national interest as being associated with the life of William Shakespeare, or his wife or parents'.

The constitution and statutory objects of the Trust as laid down in 1891 remained unchanged until an amendment to the Shakespeare Birthplace, etc., Trust Act in 1930 widened the constitution of the governing body so as to include representative trustees appointed by the Universities of Oxford, Cambridge, London and Birmingham, in addition to certain *ex-officio* trustees and life trustees. At the same time further powers and responsibilities of an educational character were added.

After the early difficult years, the Birthplace Trust entered on a period of consolidation and steady growth. In 1892 the Trustees purchased Anne Hathaway's Cottage at Shottery, which had remained until that time in the ownership and occupation of descendants of the Hathaway family. Visitors making their pilgrimage to the Birthplace and the Cottage increased almost year by year. Whereas in 1869 visitors admitted to the Birthplace numbered just over 6,000, following the turn of the century the average yearly attendance rose to 40,000. By 1927–8 this figure had reached 100,000, while Anne Hathaway's Cottage had, by this time, also come to attract an annual patronage of about two-thirds of this number. The international appeal of Shakespeare was evidenced by the fact that the visitors from overseas included representatives of no fewer than seventy nationalities. Meanwhile, improvements were carried out at New Place: first, in 1912, the restoration of Nash's House (New Place Museum) to its Tudor appearance; and then the re-presentation of the gardens, particularly the Knott garden, on Elizabethan lines in 1920. Within a short time New Place Museum came to fulfil the role of the town's museum of local history and archaeology. A further important development occurred in 1930 when the Trust was able to acquire Mary Arden's House (Shakespeare's mother's home) at Wilmcote for preservation as a memorial and to establish in its barns and outbuildings a museum of old Warwickshire farming implements and local bygones. In this same year the Trustees also bought the land at Welcombe which Shakespeare himself had originally owned.

The Birthplace museum and library in the 1880s

Expansion

The Trust's resources for the student and scholar also began to grow. Gifts and purchases of books, records and museum items were made in increasing numbers. The Trust had appointed its first part-time Secretary in 1866, and its first Librarian in 1873. Its first full-time Secretary and Librarian, Richard Savage, held office from 1886 to 1910 and was succeeded by F. C. Wellstood (1910–42), whose knowledge and enthusiasm as an antiquary and record-keeper led to important accessions of records and archaeological material. Meanwhile, space inside the Birthplace itself had proved inadequate to accommodate the Trust's growing collections. In 1903 two cottages adjoining the Birthplace garden on its eastern boundary, which were occupied by the Horneby family during Shakespeare's lifetime, were presented to the Trustees by Andrew Carnegie for use as offices, and ten years later an adjoining building at the rear was partly reconstructed to accommodate the library. A new block of strongrooms for the storage of records was added in 1936. These improved facilities ensured the further continued growth and use of the library and archives collections.

The war years (1939–45) produced conditions of particular difficulty for the Trust. Although the Shakespearian properties were kept open, the number of visitors dwindled year by year with a consequent serious reduction in the Trust's income. Only the absolute minimum of repairs and maintenance work was undertaken, but even so the Trustees found it necessary to draw on their slender financial reserves to meet running costs. All the valuable exhibits were removed for safe-keeping. Some members of the staff left to undertake war duties and the Secretary and Librarian, Mr F. C. Wellstood, died in 1942. It was not until the end of hostilities approached that members of the armed forces – particularly our American and Commonwealth allies – began to swell the number of visitors to the properties again.

The immediate post-war period similarly presented problems of great difficulty. Within a short time it became apparent that social and economic conditions had changed and were likely to continue to change. A considerable programme of deferred repairs to the properties awaited attention; the Trust's financial resources were limited; new staff had to be recruited. Indeed there was an urgent need to overhaul all aspects of the Trust's administration and activities and to devise new ways of interpreting the objects of the Trust to meet the changed conditions.

In 1946 Sir Archibald Flower, who had guided the affairs of the Trust and the Shakespeare Memorial Theatre for many years, was succeeded as Chairman by his son, Sir Fordham; and under the guidance of its new Director (Dr Levi Fox), appointed the previous year, the Trustees embarked with enthusiasm upon a programme of reappraisal, reorganisation and expansion which culminated in the world-wide celebration of the 400th anniversary of Shakespeare's birth in 1964 and the opening of the Shakespeare Centre.

The Shakespeare Birthplace Trust Act of 1961 was promoted to acknowledge and provide for the expanding role of the Trust in the post-war period. It re-defined and extended the objects of the institution to include the promotion of the appreciation and study of the works of William Shakespeare in every part of the world; the preservation of the Birthplace and the other Shakespearian properties; and the maintenance of the Trust's collections. Considerably extended responsibilities of an educational and academic nature were added and further powers conferred upon the Trustees to acquire properties for the purpose of conserving the character of Shakespeare's Stratford. The Trust's constitution was also revised so as to widen the representation of the governing body. This now comprises nine *ex-officio* Trustees, twelve Life Trustees, five local Trustees and ten Representative Trustees appointed by universities and bodies with similar interests.

The Last Twenty-five Years

During the past twenty-five years each of the Shakespearian properties has received detailed attention, not only for the purpose of ensuring the conservation of the structure, but also with the object of enhancing the interest of each building and its contents for the visitor. Indeed, the aim has been to present the Shakespearian properties in a manner calculated generally to advance knowledge and appreciation of the life, works and times of Shakespeare. In 1949 the Birthplace itself, which up till that time was still Victorian in its appearance and presentation, underwent a thorough overhaul. All the rooms of the house, including the bedroom, whose whitewashed walls and ceilings were covered with the signatures of visitors, were re-decorated and a number of long overdue improvements were carried out (for instance lighting and heating), and considerable changes in the arrangements of furnishings and the display of exhibits were made. In the spring of the following year, 1950, Their Majesties King George VI and Queen Elizabeth, with Her Royal Highness Princess Margaret, visited Shakespeare's Birthplace; and seven years later Her Majesty Queen Elizabeth II, accompanied by H.R.H. the Duke of Edinburgh, paid a similar visit.

It was towards the end of 1949 that the Trustees took the bold decision to borrow money to buy Hall's Croft, the home of Shakespeare's daughter Susanna, which up till then had remained in private ownership. Though much neglected, the basic fabric of the house was sound, but an expensive and intricate programme of restoration had to be undertaken. The garden was re-designed and planted and the house opened in 1951 as one of the attractions of the Festival of Britain year. The Festival Club at Hall's Croft was also established at that time.

In 1954–5 long overdue repairs and improvements to Nash's House (New Place Museum) were carried out, followed by considerable changes in the presentation of the interior. The ground-floor rooms were laid out to give an impression of the background of domestic life in Shakespeare's England, while the first-floor rooms were re-equipped to give a more formal display of exhibits illustrating local history and archaeology. Meanwhile, considerable improvements had been effected in and around Anne Hathaway's Cottage. Here, as at the other properties, new interest was imparted to the gardens by re-designing layouts and undertaking new planting. Trees have always received special attention, and the Trustees can claim credit for having planted an area of woodland (oak and spruce) at Shottery as a long-term forestry project. This lies alongside a car park provided for visitors to Anne Hathaway's Cottage; a coach park has also been provided. In a similar manner Mary Arden's House has been subjected to a number of improvements, all designed to enhance the interest of the farmhouse and its barns, and new outbuildings have been added to provide more adequate accommodation for the farming museum assembled there.

It is not surprising that during this same period adaptations to the Trust's office accommodation had to be undertaken and additional storage space sought for the library and records. The need for more commodious premises to meet the growing demands of the Trust's expanding administration, and of its educational and academic activities, was already being felt by the middle of the 1950s, and in 1957 a decision was taken to plan a new Shakespeare Centre which would serve both as the future headquarters of the Trust and as a library and study centre. This subsequently became the Birthplace Trust's commemorative project to mark the 400th anniversary of Shakespeare's birth, and with the help of Shakespeare lovers all over the world the new Centre came into existence and has been in use since 1964.

International Role

The growth in the international appreciation of the Shakespearian properties during the past quarter of a century has been remarkable. In 1945 the total number of visitors to the Birthplace was 78,000; by 1950 it had risen to nearly 200,000; and in 1963 a quarter of a million was reached. In 1964 the Shakespeare anniversary year's total of 320,000 appeared to set a record unlikely to be exceeded; but within two years it had been, and by 1971 the figure had risen to 425,000. At Anne Hathaway's Cottage attendances increased from 85,000 in 1947 to 344,000 in 1971, and there were also appreciable increases in the case of New Place, Mary Arden's House and Hall's Croft. Altogether a total of 964,545 visitors were admitted to the five Shakespearian properties during 1971, of which number at least 65 per cent came from overseas, representing over a hundred different nationalities.

The money derived from visitors' admission fees constitutes the major part of the annual income of the Trust, which receives no direct financial support from the Government or the local authority. As a registered charity the Trust enjoys exemption from tax but unfortunately it has no endowment fund to guarantee its financial stability. There have been occasions in the history of the Trust when income has been barely adequate to meet the needs of the institution and public appeals were launched for the Hall's Croft and Shakespeare Centre projects. Maintenance and running costs of the properties are higher than is generally realised, while appreciable funds are needed to develop the Trust's collections, to make possible its expanding educational activities, and to finance the purchase of properties to safeguard the character of the town.

Over the years the Trust has become the owner of considerable properties. In Henley Street the Birthplace itself is safeguarded by the Trust's ownership of adjacent business premises, and at Shottery nearly all the properties around Anne Hathaway's Cottage have been acquired to provide a buffer against undesirable development. Mary Arden's House and Hall's Croft are similarly protected, while the Trust's ownership of park land at Welcombe (originally owned by Shakespeare) with the adjoining Hill estate, guarantees the preservation of the Warwick Road approach to Stratford as a green belt.

It is against this background of concern for the conservation of the character and atmosphere of Shakespeare's Stratford that the Trust's activities in the educational, cultural and academic spheres have developed, particularly during the last twenty years. Talks and lectures are provided for school and college groups and courses of study arranged in co-operation with the University of Birmingham, the British Council and the Royal Shakespeare Theatre. Exhibitions are now regularly arranged as a means of disseminating knowledge of Shakespeare's life and times, and every possible encouragement is given to researchers using the library, archives and other collections. The Trustees sponsor the issue of publications dealing with their properties and collections and sell books, visual aids and commemorative items relating to Shakespeare. They also organise an annual Festival of Poetry and a music programme.

There are numerous other ways in which the Birthplace Trust does honour to Shakespeare: by linking together Shakespeare lovers throughout the world, whether groups or individuals, in an organisation of Friends; by acting as a kind of central clearing house for enquiries from this country and overseas covering almost every aspect of Shakespearian study and production, local history, genealogy and antiquities generally; and by assuming responsibility for organising the celebrations which are held each year on Shakespeare's birthday (23 April). From small beginnings designed to give Stratford people an opportunity to pay tribute to their great townsman, these celebrations have now become a unique international occasion.

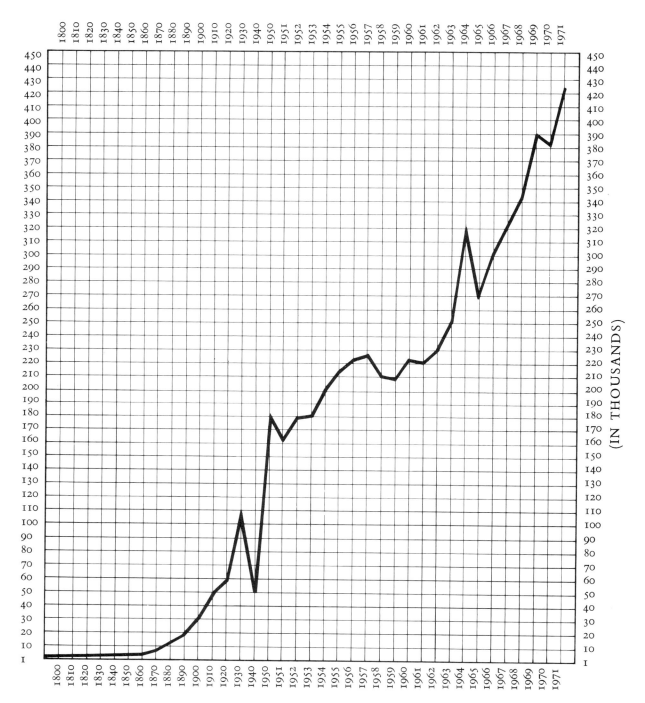

CHART SHOWING NUMBERS OF VISITORS
TO SHAKESPEARE'S BIRTHPLACE 1800–1971
(IN THOUSANDS)

The Shakespeare Centre

It is particularly appropriate that the new head-quarters of the Trust, the Shakespeare Centre, should have been built on a site overlooking the garden of Shakespeare's Birthplace. The project was conceived as a kind of international birthday present to commemorate the 400th anniversary of Shakespeare's birth and was made possible by the gifts of Shakespeare lovers of many countries. The foundation stone was laid by H.R.H. Princess Alexandra of Kent on 28 June 1962 and the Centre was officially opened on the eve of the 400th anniversary, 22 April 1964, by the Hon. Eugene R. Black, Chairman of the American 1964 Shakespeare Committee. Among the many distinguished visitors during 1964 were H.R.H. The Prince Philip, Duke of Edinburgh, and H.M. Queen Elizabeth The Queen Mother.

As a building Nikolaus Pevsner has described the Centre as 'a very handsome job and highly praiseworthy because so entirely uncompromising in so hallowed a spot'. Designed by Laurence Williams, the Trust's architect, the Centre is modern in conception and design but makes liberal use of traditional materials, including granite, marble, hand-made brick, concrete, bronze, wood, glass and leather. Carefully chosen timbers, especially cherry wood, give a distinctive character to the interior, blending with specially designed carpets and curtains, furniture and artistic embellishments to produce a strikingly modern yet dignified and restful atmosphere conducive to study and research.

A bronze relief by Douglas Wain-Hobson at the front of the Centre in Henley Street symbolises the influence of Shakespeare encircling the world, and flanking the entrance a large black granite panel, carved by John Skelton, labels the building. The entrance vestibule itself is enclosed by a series of glass panels engraved with life-size figures of well-known Shakespearian characters by John Hutton, while a bronze full-figure statue of Shakespeare, also by Douglas Wain-Hobson, provides a striking focal point in the entrance hall.

From this central point internal perambulation for the public and staff flows naturally to the various rooms providing for the library and academic work of the Trust. On the ground floor there is provision for readers, library staff and lecture and exhibition facilities. The Stratford room – so called because contributions from Stratfordians largely paid for its furnishings – is a general-purpose lecture room or seminar which is also used for exhibitions and as a meeting place for local societies.

Apart from a conference room which is used for meetings of the Trustees and other purposes, the first-floor accommodation is devoted entirely to offices for the Director and the headquarters staff of the Trust. Name-plates associated with

H.R.H Princess Alexandra laying the foundation stone in 1962

Official opening of the Shakespeare Centre by the Hon. Eugene R. Black, 22 April 1964

the windows in the conference room and other rooms on this floor emphasise the interest in Shakespeare that exists throughout the world in that they record the names of the countries which contributed in money or kind to the Shakespeare Centre project.

The provision and equipment of the library portion of the building was made possible by the generosity of the Nuffield Foundation. The carpeted reading room has the atmosphere of a large, comfortable private study, its walls being lined with individual desks each provided with lighting and shelves, and with windows above. Natural lighting is increased by a glass dome above a central reading table. An unusual artistic feature in the form of a curved wood panel, made in five different timbers to give depth and variety of colour effect, runs the whole length of the west wall. It is carved with the names of Shakespeare and many of his contemporaries and is the work of Mrs Nicolette Gray, a distinguished authority on the art of architectural lettering. Readers may consult general reference works kept on open shelves in the reading room, but other books and library materials are brought from storage in the basement in response to request slips filled in after consulting the catalogue and indexes.

The basement stacks, approached either by lift or stairway, are designed to give the maximum security; they are proofed against fire, and temperatures suited to the proper care of books are maintained. All the equipment is specially designed, steel shelving with vertical matching files, drawers and cabinets providing for the storage of photographs, drawings, playbills and theatrical production records. Very rare books and valuable items are kept in an air-conditioned strongroom. Special provision is made for students working on long-term projects or wishing to use typewriters or tape recorders, and there are also facilities for microtext reading and for photographic reproduction work.

Nicolette Gray's carved panel

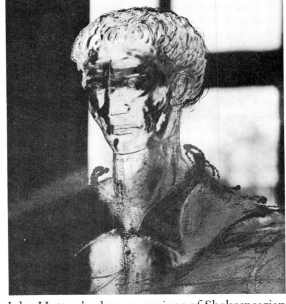

John Hutton's glass engravings of Shakespearian characters: Hamlet (*above*)

The reading room

Richard III

Titania

Since 1969 supplementary accommodation for the use of student groups has been provided in an annexe in a building immediately adjacent to the Centre.

Shakespeare's Birthplace

No record of the erection of the Birthplace survives, but architectural features suggest that the greater part of it was built in the late fifteenth or early sixteenth centuries. Like most of the old houses of Stratford-upon-Avon it was a product of local materials: timber from the nearby Forest of Arden and blue-grey stone from Wilmcote, the village where Shakespeare's mother lived as a girl nearly four miles from the town.

The building consists of a low foundation wall of stone on which is erected a framing of oak

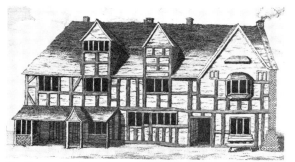

R. Greene's drawing of the Birthplace, 1769

The kitchen

beams, the spaces between the timbers being filled in with wattle and daub and the structure consolidated by a massive stone chimney stack in the centre and a raftered roof. The timbers on the lower frontage are of the early, close-studded type, about nine inches wide and the same distance apart, with rectangular panels in the upper storey.

Though it has suffered some changes and necessary restoration the property bears substantially the same appearance as in the earliest surviving representation of it (*illustrated left*), and having regard to its age contains a good deal of the original timber framing. Though now detached, the Birthplace originally formed part of a continuous frontage of houses and shops abutting on to Henley Street. The buildings formerly on either side were demolished in 1857 to diminish fire risk.

There is documentary proof that John Shakespeare, William's father, was living in Henley Street as early as 1552, and records survive which prove that the premises were occupied and owned by him. Tradition assigns the western portion of the building as the poet's birthplace. At that time the Birthplace property consisted of two separate buildings, the one being the Shakespeare family's home, and the other a shop or warehouse adjoining, also owned by John Shakespeare and used in connection with his trade as a glover and wool dealer.

The house portion, comprising living room, kitchen, cellar, the Birthroom and other bedrooms, is furnished in the style of Elizabethan and Jacobean times with items comparable to those described in inventories of the furnishings of middle-class homes in Shakespeare's Stratford. The remainder of the building is equipped as a museum for the display of documentation relating to the history and association of the building and exhibits illustrating the parentage, career, works, sources, portraiture and growing appreciation of the poet.

The Birthplace from Henley Street

The traditional Birthroom

New Place

One of the indisputable facts about Shakespeare is that when he was approaching the peak of his fame and success as a playwright in London he purchased the house in Stratford-upon-Avon known as New Place. That occurred in 1597 and the legal document (*illustrated opposite*) transferring the property to the poet for the sum of £60 is preserved among the records of the Shakespeare Birthplace Trust.

New Place, standing at the corner of Chapel Street and Chapel Lane, was originally built towards the end of the fifteenth century by Hugh Clopton, a native and benefactor of Stratford who became Lord Mayor of London. Described by John Leland, who visited the town about 1540, as a 'pretty house of brick and timber', it was evidently a large, half-timbered structure of the type common in Tudor Stratford. It had a court

The Knott garden with its interlaced beds of herbs and flowers

in front and had barns and spacious gardens and orchard attached.

Evidence suggests that, following his purchase of New Place, Shakespeare gradually established himself as a townsman of Stratford, although continuing to live and work in London until 1610, when he settled permanently at New Place to live with his family. Various documents illustrate the poet's relations with his fellow townsmen, several of whom were his intimate friends. Shakespeare died at New Place on 23 April 1616, after entertaining Jonson and Drayton, it is said. He bequeathed New Place to his elder daughter Susanna, wife of Dr John Hall, and it is probable that Shakespeare's widow lived with the Halls there until her death in 1623. Queen Henrietta Maria, Charles I's queen, stayed at New Place for three days in 1643 as the guest of Susanna Hall.

Subsequently New Place was owned by Elizabeth Hall, the poet's granddaughter, who married Thomas Nash, and as her second husband, Sir John Barnard of Abington, Northamptonshire. Following her death and that of her husband, New Place was sold in 1675 to Sir Edward Walker, Garter King of Arms, and passed through the marriage of his daughter back into the Clopton family. Sir John Clopton entirely re-built the house in 1702 and the only pictorial record of the original New Place which Shakespeare knew is a sketch of the frontage (*reproduced opposite*) drawn some forty years afterwards.

By the middle of the eighteenth century visitors wishing to see the mulberry tree at New Place, said to have been planted by Shakespeare himself, had become so numerous as to cause annoyance to the then owner of the property, the Reverend Francis Gastrell, who in consequence had the tree cut down in 1756. Three years later he became involved in a quarrel with the town authorities, following which he caused the house itself to be demolished. The site containing the foundations of the original New Place thus left vacant became annexed to Nash's House next door (Thomas Nash married Shakespeare's granddaughter, Elizabeth Hall), as its garden and belonged to various owners until 1862, when the whole property was purchased for preservation as a national memorial to the poet and was later vested in the Shakespeare Birthplace Trust.

Adjoining the foundations is the Knott garden which is a replica of an enclosed Elizabethan garden, and beyond is the great garden which formed the original orchard and kitchen garden attached to New Place.

Legal document transferring property to Shakespeare for the sum of £60

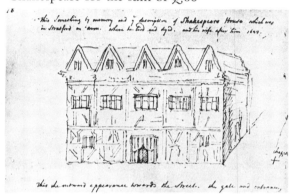

The earliest surviving drawing of New Place

Nash's House, overlooking the foundations of New Place, now a museum of local history

Anne Hathaway's Cottage

Situated at Shottery just over a mile from the centre of the town, Anne Hathaway's Cottage closely rivals Shakespeare's Birthplace in its appeal to the tourist and literary pilgrim. Anne, daughter of Richard Hathaway, was born here in 1556. She married William Shakespeare in 1582 and outlived him by seven years.

At that time Shottery was little more than a cluster of homesteads standing on the fringe of the forest, and it has been suggested that Shakespeare's description of the situation of Celia's home in *As You Like It* was inspired by the poet's recollections of his wife's early home.

Visitors are invariably impressed by the size of this picturesque timber-framed building, with its irregular walls, high-pitched thatched roof and tiny latticed windows. It is indeed much more than what a 'cottage' is usually expected to be and this is explained by the fact that it was originally a twelve-roomed farmhouse, known as Hewlands, which was the home of the Hathaways, who were a well-respected substantial yeoman family, long established in Shottery and

The Cottage from the orchard

Stratford. John Hathaway, for instance, served as a constable of the parish in 1520 and references in local records from this time substantiate the association of members of the Hathaway family with Hewlands and their participation in farming activities.

Apart from repairs carried out following a fire which damaged part of the property in 1969, the fabric has suffered remarkably little restoration. Much of it is of sixteenth- and seventeenth-century work but the oldest part dates back to the fifteenth century. Inside the house may be seen a pair of curved oak timbers or 'crucks', pegged together at the top, which was one of the earliest constructional methods used in house building in this country. Built on foundations of stone, the timber-framed walls consist mostly of wattle and daub panels finished with hair plaster inside, though in some cases brick of later date has been substituted. The central chimney stack was rebuilt in 1697 and bears the initials of John Hathaway.

The principal rooms on the ground floor comprise the living room, or the 'hall' as it was called in Shakespeare's day, with its original panelling, dresser and open chimney corner; the kitchen with its old bake-oven still intact; and the dairy or buttery, an essential adjunct to any farmhouse. Upstairs there are six rooms, all formerly used as bedrooms or storerooms, running the whole length of the building, the principal chamber containing the famous Hathaway bedstead of late Elizabethan date.

Anne Hathaway's Cottage remained in the ownership and occupation of descendants of the Hathaways until the Birthplace Trust bought it in 1892. Most of the present furnishings of the Cottage belonged to successive generations of the family, though a few representative pieces of period furniture have been added. The old English garden, with the orchard adjoining, provides an almost perfect setting for this architectural gem.

The 'crucks' construction

The hall with the built-in dresser

The Cottage in its garden setting

Hall's Croft

Born in 1575, the son of William Hall, a Bedfordshire doctor, John Hall studied at Queens' College, Cambridge, and took his degree of Master of Arts in 1597. Subsequently he pursued his medical studies abroad, and about 1600, for reasons not definitely known, he settled in Stratford-upon-Avon and began to practise as a doctor. In 1607 he married Susanna Shakespeare, the poet's daughter, and the following year their only daughter Elizabeth was born. The Halls resided at Hall's Croft until after Shakespeare's death in 1616, when the family moved to New Place. Dr Hall died in 1635 and Susanna in 1649.

From an architectural point of view Hall's Croft displays all the essential characteristics of the half-timbered town houses common in Stratford-upon-Avon in Shakespeare's time. Built on a stone foundation, the structure is of substantial oak timber-framing, lath and plaster, with a tiled roof of many gables surmounted by picturesque chimney stacks. The northern portion of the building dates back to the early sixteenth century: the lower storey has close-set timber-framing, and the overhanging upper

Dr Hall's dispensary

floor rests on shaped brackets carved from the upright posts. This was evidently the original house, a small, compact dwelling with outbuildings at the rear, which was enlarged at the beginning of the seventeenth century, probably by Dr Hall himself, into a more commodious residence. The present entrance hall, staircase and landing were built at that time to link the original house with rooms added on the south side at the front and with an improved kitchen at the rear.

Further additions and alterations were made during the eighteenth and nineteenth centuries. Some of these, such as the addition of bay windows to the frontage and the insertion of larger windows in various rooms, seriously weakened the structure. Thus, when Hall's Croft was purchased for preservation by the Birthplace Trust in 1949, a comprehensive overhaul of the fabric had to be undertaken and certain spoliations of later date removed in order to restore the plan and elevations of the house as near as possible to what they were in Dr Hall's time.

The rooms are now furnished in the style of a middle-class town house of the period and contain some fine pieces of Tudor and Jacobean date. Dr Hall's dispensary is equipped as a contemporary consulting-room, complete with apothecaries' jars for medicines, herbs and pills, pestles and mortars, herbals and the like; the kitchen, with its open hearth and medley of pots and cooking utensils, still gives the impression of having been the hub of the domestic arrangements of the household.

Hall's Croft has a spacious walled garden which – as the term 'Croft' suggests – no doubt originally comprised both a garden for flowers and herbs and a kitchen garden and orchard. The present layout was designed in 1950; it seeks to portray something of the formality of gardens of Shakespeare's day and at the same time to create the intimate atmosphere of a homely garden full of familiar trees, flowers and shrubs.

Hall's Croft from Old Town

The parlour

The kitchen

23

Mary Arden's House

This Tudor farmstead, the home of Shakespeare's mother, Mary Arden, was occupied until 1930, when the Birthplace Trust acquired it for preservation. Situated at Wilmcote, just over three miles from Stratford, the farmhouse stands back slightly from the roadway behind a wall enclosing quaint, shaped hedges of box. The timbered frontage is of striking size and proportions. Most of the structure is of early sixteenth-century date. The outer walls are of substantial timber-framing standing on a stone foundation about three feet from the ground. The timber came from the Forest of Arden nearby and the stone was quarried in Wilmcote itself. At the front the upright timbers are set close together, but at the back the framing is at wider intervals, forming large panels which were originally filled in with clay on wattle. The roof, with its picturesque dormer windows, is covered with hand-made tiles.

The Ardens, who lived here in the sixteenth century, came of an old and leading county family. Robert Arden had eight daughters, Mary marrying John Shakespeare of Snitterfield, the poet's father, in 1557. An inventory of Robert Arden's goods taken after his death in 1556 shows the main contents and stock of his farmstead to have included a variety of furniture comprising tables, forms, benches, coffers and cupboards; beds, bedding, linen and painted cloths; copper pans, brass pots, candlesticks and cooking utensils; a quern, kneading trough and vessels for milking and brewing; various tools; wheat and straw in the barns; carts, ploughs and harrows; and livestock – all valued at £77 11s. 10d. Such was the background of the early years of Shakespeare's mother.

It is most fortunate that continued occupation of the Arden farmstead by farmers ensured its preservation substantially in its original condition. The plan of the house consists of a central passage or entrance lobby with doors at both front and back, dividing the kitchen on the one side from the hall, which served as the principal living apartment, on the other. Originally open to the roof, the hall was subsequently converted into two storeys by the insertion of a floor supported by a massive beam, and another wing was added at the farther end. In other respects the house bears all the characteristics of the home of a yeoman farmer of Shakespeare's day.

At the rear of the house, a stretch of lawn, with borders of herbaceous flowers, now occupies the space of the original farmyard, but the barns, dovecote, cowsheds and outbuildings are preserved intact. They now accommodate a farming museum of old agricultural implements and other reminders of rural life

The stone dovecote

The farm's water supply

Front view of Mary Arden's House

The House from the farmyard

The Library

The beginnings of the library date back to 1862 when a number of books were assembled, together with museum items, in the part of the Birthplace property which had formerly been the Swan and Maidenhead inn. The idea of the early Trustees was to provide a collection of source material, comprising books, manuscripts, pictures and museum items, illustrative of the life, times and works of Shakespeare. A first *Brief guide to the Shakespeare Library and Museum, Stratford-upon-Avon*, price one penny, was produced in 1865, and a more elaborate *Catalogue of the books, manuscripts, works of art, antiquities and relics* . . . running to 171 pages in 1868. Both publications were evidently inspired by the Shakespearian scholar, J. O. Halliwell-Phillipps, who was not only generous with his own gifts but who was active in influencing others to present or deposit useful items. Charles Jackman was appointed Librarian in 1873 and was succeeded by Bruce Tyndall (1880–2). Rules for the consultation of books and manuscripts were adopted by the Trustees in 1878 and 1881.

It was at this time that the Shakespeare Memorial in Waterside, inspired and generously supported by Charles Edward Flower, came into existence: the theatre was opened in 1879 and was followed the next year by the memorial library and picture gallery. The object was to provide a collection of editions of Shakespeare's plays as the nucleus of a specialised library of dramatic literature, acting editions, prompt copies and theatrical material. In spite of the competing attraction of this second Shakespeare collection in the town the Birthplace library continued to develop and under the guidance of Richard Savage, and later of Frederick Wellstood, accessions of considerable importance were acquired. In particular, copies of all the folios, a number of quartos and most of the early editions of Shakespeare's plays were secured, as well as a representative selection of works of Shakespeare's period. Some of the more interesting books were

exhibited in the Birthplace itself and were described in the *Catalogue of the Books, Manuscripts, Works of Art, Antiquities and Relics exhibited in Shakespeare's Birthplace* first compiled by Richard Savage in 1910, and then revised by Frederick Wellstood and re-issued at intervals down to 1944.

Meanwhile, although separated physically, the Birthplace and Theatre libraries came to be regarded as complementary, rather than independent collections, and their combined resources came to be increasingly used by scholars and research students. In 1947 the Birthplace library underwent considerable re-organisation and it was at this time that the Director of the Trust assumed responsibility for the supervision of the Theatre library. Changes were introduced in classification and cataloguing as a preliminary to the ultimate amalgamation of the two related collections. This finally became possible when the new Shakespeare Centre was built: in 1964 the Birthplace and Theatre libraries were merged and since then they have been completely re-organised and developed as a unified collection.

The library collections contain some 25,000 volumes, many thousands of pamphlets and Shakespearian items, including an unusually large number associated with famous scholars and actors. The main subject categories are: English books published between 1529 and 1640; Shakespeare and Shakespeariana; drama and dramatic history and criticism other than Shakespeare, particularly Elizabethan and Jacobean; theatrical history and biography, including some foreign theatrical history and biography; local history and topography, particularly of Stratford-upon-Avon and Warwickshire; and miscellaneous, such as pictorial material, heraldry, costume, autographs, historical background.

The Stratford collections of Shakespeariana are much richer than is generally appreciated. Here are copies not only of the first four folios, but of several early and later quartos together with practically every other complete edition of the poet's works published, as well as of editions of individual plays. The latter include a representative selection of early acting editions and a number of prompt copies associated with nineteenth-century actors. Shakesperian prompt books include a number of early nineteenth-century Covent Garden Theatre books. Translations of complete works and of individual plays are also collected.

On the biographical side the collections contain copies of early works containing allusions to Shakespeare as well as published lives from Nathan Drake to the present day. General criticism and criticism of plays include publications ranging from the works of contemporaries of Shakespeare to present-day studies. There is a representative selection of drama and dramatic history and criticism with some emphasis on seventeenth- and eighteenth-century editions.

Theatrical history and biography occupy an important place. Naturally the emphasis again is on the history of Shakespearian production, though theatrical memoirs, biography and history in general are well represented. Playbills include collections of London and provincial theatres during the nineteenth century, as well as of Shakespeare playbills from the time of Garrick to the present day. There is also a collection of programmes of productions both in this country and abroad together with prints and photographs of actors in Shakespearian roles. Special mention should be made of the Bram Stoker collection

of Irving material, consisting of portfolios containing programmes, photographs, notices, caricatures and the like for various seasons, and of boxes containing programmes, playbills, letters, proof copies of editions of plays arranged by Irving, speeches, agreements, and sundry material, including much which pre-dates Stoker's association with Irving.

The archives of Stratford's own festival history and of the Royal Shakespeare Theatre (formerly the Shakespeare Memorial Theatre) constitute one of the specialities of the library. Much of the documentation of the successive Shakespeare festivals from the Garrick Jubilee of 1769 onwards is here, together with prints and curios associated with particular festivals. The records of the Royal Shakespeare Theatre itself comprise press cuttings books from 1874 when the movement for the Shakespeare Memorial started; playbills from the opening performances of 1879 onwards; prompt copies from 1922 (with a few gaps) to date, including productions presented at the Aldwych Theatre; photographs of actors in festival productions and in some cases of sets; designs for scenery and costumes; and a collection of gramophone records and orchestral parts of incidental music for particular productions.

The local history and topographical sections constitute another field of subject-matter in which the library is particularly strong. All aspects of the history of Warwickshire, and especially of Stratford-upon-Avon, are covered; and there are general works of reference and source books for use in conjunction with the manuscript material in the Trust's records office.

Archives

The preservation of records illustrating the poet's life and period, and the history and social life of Stratford-upon-Avon, was from the beginning regarded as an integral part of the function of the Birthplace library and museum. Among early acquisitions were the manuscript collections of Robert Bell Wheler (1785–1857), the historian of Stratford, and the transcripts and drawings of Captain James Saunders (d. 1830). In 1862 the ancient borough records of Stratford-upon-Avon were transferred from the Guildhall to a room in the Birthplace equipped for their storage (the old 'record room' over the present entrance). Within twenty years the Birthplace collections of archive material had grown appreciably and when J. C. Jeaffreson reported on them in 1883 he called attention to certain Gunpowder Plot documents in the Wheler MSS., and 'some interesting letters and memoranda touching the successive Shakespeare Centenary Festivals'. Between 1884 and 1894 G. F. Warner, an assistant in the Department of Manuscripts at the British Museum, undertook the calendaring of documents for the Trust.

Towards the end of the century an important step was taken towards the preservation of local genealogical source material by the copying of parish registers and other local records, including monumental inscriptions; this was largely due, no doubt, to the quest for information about Shakespeare and his family. In pursuit of this work Richard Savage visited many neighbouring parishes, and incumbents and officials as far afield as Worcester. Another worker in this field, J. Harvey Bloom, made during the years 1900–10 a comprehensive local collection of parochial transcripts and notes now in the Trust's collections, which are constantly in use by students of family history.

Further accessions and improvements in the organisation of the library and archive collections were inspired by Sir Sidney Lee, editor of the *Dictionary of National Biography*, who was

Chairman of the Executive Committee of the Trust from 1903 to 1926. The first complete revision of the *Catalogue* since 1868, containing notes on the history of books, manuscripts and objects exhibited in the Birthplace, was completed in 1910. Shortly afterwards the Corporation records and other manuscripts were transferred from the old record room in the Birthplace building itself to a new strongroom and library reconstructed from the former custodian's cottage situated on the boundary of the Birthplace garden. In May 1915 the Royal Commission on Public Records, of which Sir Sidney was a member, visited Stratford-upon-Avon and inspected the borough archives, and those of the Trust, in the new strongroom. F. C. Wellstood had prepared lists of both sets of documents; his summary statement (1915) describes the Birthplace collections as consisting at that time of 256 bound volumes and about 5,600 other documents, dealing with the history and antiquities of Stratford-upon-Avon and surrounding country, and with the life and work of Shakespeare.

With the changing conditions that followed the end of the First World War, the amended property laws and the resulting dispersal of private records, the Birthplace library at Stratford came near to fulfilling the purpose of a general record repository for south-west Warwickshire and parts of adjoining counties. Considerable accessions of manuscript material accrued at this time, including the first of the larger family collections deposited, that of Lord Willoughby de Broke. In 1931 the Master of the Rolls approved the Birthplace library as a repository for manorial records, thus giving official sanction to its development as a general record repository. Within little more than a year the Trustees were able to record the deposit of 402 Warwickshire court rolls by Major Charles Gregory-Hood and 206 court rolls of the manor of Snitterfield by Mr Robert Trevelyan and Mr Thomas Place, besides other documents. The total number of manorial documents received by 1935 was 2,751; and by 1937, 5,564. One of the most substantial deposits of manorial documents was that made by Sir Robert Throckmorton, Bt.

Changes affecting accommodation and personnel naturally accompanied these developments. A new fireproof block, of three strong-rooms for records storage, was added in 1936 and opened in 1937. So far as staff is concerned, up to the early 1930s, apart from secretarial assistance, the secretary and librarian had usually worked single-handed on the archives, but, as a result of a suggestion thrown out by Lord Hanworth in 1933, an assistant archivist with legal training was appointed in 1934. The war years saw continued accessions of records, augmented occasionally by material retrieved from salvage drives. Lord Leigh of Stoneleigh Abbey deposited most of his collection in this period, including one consignment of eighty-two trunks and boxes. Another large family collection received shortly after the war was the Archer collection deposited by the Earl of Plymouth from Hewell Grange. The deposits of Major Charles Gregory-Hood were continued in the post-war period with additional deposits by his son, Lt.-Col. Alexander Gregory-Hood. Several accumulations from solicitors' offices have also been received and other items acquired by purchase during this period. In 1959 the probate records of the peculiar courts of Stratford-upon-Avon and Hampton Lucy were transferred to the Birthplace records office from the District Probate Registry, Birmingham. More recently the Vicar and Churchwardens of Holy Trinity Church have deposited the parish records of Stratford.

The records of Stratford-upon-Avon are remarkably complete and well preserved, and have attracted attention as a Shakespearian quarry at least from the days of Malone. Of the Trust's foundation collections, that of Wheler contains unique Shakespearian documents such as the Quyney letter and material from various local sources covering the period 1289–c. 1850; the Saunders collection includes transcripts of medieval documents in Warwickshire archives that Captain James Saunders had access to between 1800 and 1810, and several hundred Warwickshire drawings of the same period; the Hunt collection contains local papers and correspondence, 1596–c.1860, including some of

Garrick's letters relating to the Stratford Jubilee, 1769; and Halliwell-Phillipps's collection, consisting chiefly of printed material and volumes of notes on Shakespeare's plays.

Estate and family collections include the Compton Verney and Chesterton deeds and papers of Lord Willoughby de Broke; the Stoneleigh collection deposited by Lord Leigh; the Stivichall collection of Lt.-Col. Alexander Gregory-Hood; the Coughton collection consisting of court rolls of twenty manors and deeds of various counties of Sir Robert Throckmorton, Bt; the Archer collection of the Earl of Plymouth; Snitterfield and Welcombe deeds and court rolls formerly of Mr Robert Trevelyan; and Baddesley Clinton deeds and papers formerly of Mr C. R. Ferrers. Manorial court rolls relating to nearly 200 manors, mostly in Warwickshire but a few in other counties are also held.

Finally, the Birthplace Trust has a considerable accumulation of its own administrative and other records, including the title-deeds of the Trust properties.

The records room.

Pictures and Prints

Apart from the portraits of Shakespeare (*see pages 76–7*) and his contemporaries, the Trust's picture and print collection falls primarily into three categories: a number of sixteenth- and seventeenth-century pictures, most of which are on display in the Shakespearian properties; a varied assortment of print and pictorial material relating to all aspects of Shakespeare's life, works and times; and a local topographical group containing items which portray the changing face of Stratford over the last 250 years.

The first category includes the portraits of prominent people associated with Stratford, such as members of the Clopton family, as well as scenes (for example, the seventeenth-century oil painting of Windsor Castle) which Shakespeare himself might have known. In the second category are to be found a number of imaginative reconstructions of scenes from Shakespeare's life, from the eighteenth century onwards. The poet's courtship of Anne Hathaway and the traditional deer-stealing episode at Charlecote have proved favourite subjects. Closely related is the collection of eighteenth- and nineteenth-century paintings, drawings and prints of famous actors and actresses playing character roles in Shakespeare's plays, and of productions and sets for the plays themselves. Taken as a whole the theatrical collection is extensive and varied. It provides an invaluable source for students of theatre history and of Shakespearian production and is kept up to date (although now with the aid of photographs) with records of modern productions.

Of Shakespearian interest also are the pictures and prints which record the successive Shakespeare Festivals that have been held at Stratford (*see pages 72–3*). By far the greatest number of items, however, relate to Stratford itself which, because of its Shakespearian associations, has always attracted artists. A picture such as Thomas Girtin's watercolour of the old Charnel House that once adjoined Holy Trinity Church has considerable artistic merit, but the majority of the pictures in the collection are more important as records. Taken together they form an important source for the history of Stratford, recording streets and buildings (such as Middle Row) that have now disappeared or visibly changed beyond recognition. Particularly important are a set of six early eighteenth-century oil paintings depicting the River Avon, Clopton Bridge, Holy Trinity Church and the mill. Local artists have also recorded Stratford's history and topography. The Reverend Joseph Greene, with his brother Richard, whose drawing of the Birthplace is the earliest representation known, were pioneers in this sphere. Among other names, that of Captain James Saunders is the most deservedly famous: his extensive collection of topographical drawings, exhibiting a remarkable precision of detail and high standard of draughtsmanship, constitutes a unique source for illustrating Stratford at the turn of the eighteenth and nineteenth centuries. His work is supplemented by a close contemporary, John Jordan, a local wheelwright and eccentric who aspired to be a poet and artist, whose drawings, if lacking the skill of Saunders are nevertheless faithful reproductions of what he saw. More impressive and accurate and carried forward into the early part of the Victorian era, were the sketches of Robert Bell Wheler, perhaps the greatest of all Stratford's antiquarians.

Early view of Clopton Bridge, published in 1795

Furniture

The fact that the Shakespearian properties are furnished and equipped as houses that were lived in greatly enhances their interest and educational value. Taken together the five historic houses accommodate an impressive and important collection of furniture of Shakespeare's period.

None of the pieces has any direct or proven association with the poet himself, though in the Birthplace a sixteenth-century school desk which came from the local Grammar School over a century ago is known by tradition as 'Shakespeare's desk'. Similarly at Anne Hathaway's Cottage the old wooden settle near to the fireplace in the hall has been pointed out from the early years of the last century as the 'courting-settle' where the young poet and Anne did their courting. Of greater significance is that Anne Hathaway's Cottage contains pieces of furniture like the Hathaway bedstead, the dining table and the dresser which have remained in the house since Shakespeare's time.

Many of the items in the Trust's furniture collection correspond closely to those listed in the inventories of the goods and chattels of Stratford tradesmen and farmers in Shakespeare's time which are preserved in the borough records. The inventory of the goods of Shakespeare's grandfather, Robert Arden of Wilmcote who died in 1556, still survives and gives a good idea of how the house of a middle-class farming family of the early Tudor period would have been furnished. What is immediately noticeable is that there were fewer items of furniture than would be usual today, and that they tended to be strictly utilitarian. Robert Arden's table, for instance, was of the trestle type, which could be easily dismantled and moved aside. Stools and benches, rather than chairs, were commonly used while coffers and chests provided storage facilities.

Styles and tastes in furniture were already changing during Shakespeare's lifetime. By the end of the sixteenth century framed tables with carved legs were replacing the earlier trestle tables in the better-class houses as seen by the excellent examples at New Place and Hall's Croft. New ideas were being introduced, such as, for instance, as indicated by the extending refectory table in the parlour of Hall's Croft, and chairs became increasingly used alongside stools and benches. Various forms of upholstery added to comfort, and by the early Jacobean period ornately carved armchairs, as illustrated by several in the Trust's collection, had become popular. The simple truckle bed had also given way in many middle-class houses to the 'half-headed' type of bed as seen in the birthroom at the Birthplace, while the more well-to-do might aspire to a carved four-poster bed such as is exhibited in the little bedroom at Hall's Croft.

Other basic items well represented in the collection are court cupboards and chests or coffers. The former include some fine specimens of the open-shelf type as well as those of more solid construction, enclosed by doors, which provided more scope for the woodcarver's embellishments. The chests range from the simple country-type elm coffer and oak chests of varying sizes with the linenfold pattern to the more pretentious and ornate specimens with richly carved front panels. Individual period pieces of special interest and rarity include an oak Tudor table with an aumbry or cupboard for storing food (*see below*), a settle-table with box seat and bobbin-turned supports, and an unusual child's high chair of 'turned' ash wood.

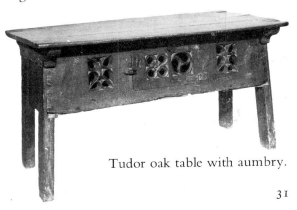

Tudor oak table with aumbry.

Museum Materials

The Trust's museum collections cover a wide range of interests and illustrate some of the many activities and responsibilities that the Trust has undertaken since its inception. One of the most important groups of items, including some of the earliest exhibits acquired by the Trust, naturally relates to Shakespeare and his associations with Stratford. Few objects that can be identified with certainty with the poet's life have survived, but a number of items associated with the Shakespearian properties and with the poet's family and friends are still in existence.

In addition to this the Trust has built up a unique collection of what may be called Shakespeariana, which holds considerable fascination for Shakespeare lovers. This category includes the many souvenirs of Shakespeare and Stratford that have been produced in an astonishing variety of forms and materials since the middle of the eighteenth century. Among the earliest are the wooden items, such as goblets, caskets, snuff-boxes and tobacco stoppers, which were carved by the celebrated local craftsman, Thomas Sharp, from the wood of Shakespeare's mulberry tree cut down in 1756. A particularly fine example of mulberry-wood carving is the oval carved medallion of Shakespeare himself worn by David Garrick at the Stratford Jubilee of 1769 (*see page 68*). Much nearer our time are the commemorative souvenirs which were produced in 1964 to mark the 400th anniversary of Shakespeare's birth. Several of these, such as the china produced by Wedgwood, the Webbs crystal glass, the handprinted tapestry panels of Tibor Reich and the Shakespeare commemorative medal designed by Paul Vincze, were sponsored by the 1964 Shakespeare Anniversary Council.

One of the objects of the Trust has also been to assemble museum material which illustrates both the national and local background of Shakespeare's period. Hence its fine collection of Elizabethan and Jacobean furniture, domestic utensils and articles of everyday use, including pottery, glassware and iron objects. For the most part these are on display in the various Shakespearian properties (New Place Museum *shown opposite*) where they help to give an impression of the everyday environment in which Shakespeare lived.

Apart from its specialised interest in all aspects of Shakespeare the Trust has increasingly come to discharge the function of a museum for local antiquities relating to the history of Stratford and the surrounding countryside. Apart from a few prehistoric items New Place Museum contains a representative collection of Roman remains from the Romano-British industrial settlement which flourished at nearby Tiddington from the first to the fifth centuries. To a later date and of considerable archaeological importance are the grave goods from two early pagan Saxon cemeteries at Stratford and Bidford-on-Avon. Among the finds from these two sites are extremely fine and rare specimens of intricately decorated Saxon jewellery and a remarkable range of personal items belonging to the Saxon warriors and their ladies.

Relatively few items relating to the medieval period of Stratford's history have survived apart from some carved oak figures which originally adorned the Gild Chapel and the Gild's muniment chest. The history of the Borough, incorporated by charter in 1553, has been better served by time, and a wide variety of borough bygones, deposited with the Trust by the Corporation of Stratford, are included in the collection. Ranging in date from the mid-sixteenth to the twentieth century, they include the early civic insignia, weapons from the borough armoury once used by the local militia, early weights and measures, and an extensive group of items relating to the maintenance of law and order in the town, culminating with the formation of the Borough Police Force.

The Trust's folk life and farming collection

is appropriately housed at Mary Arden's House (*see page 34*), as also the collection of early pharmacy jars and medical items illustrative of the period of Dr John Hall, at Hall's Croft (*see above*). Mention should also be made of the collection of coins, both of the Roman period and of Elizabethan and Jacobean times. Shakespeare medals form another specialist category which includes the latest series of Shakespeare commemorative medals which are being designed by Paul Vincze in association with the Birthplace Trust (*see page 128*).

Farming and Rural Life

When the Birthplace Trustees acquired Mary Arden's House in 1930 they decided that this property provided a particularly appropriate setting for illustrating the farming and country background into which Shakespeare was born. The various rooms of the farmhouse were accordingly furnished with pieces of period furniture, domestic utensils and the like, such as would have been found in the homes of many Warwickshire farming families in Shakespeare's time, and which included items such as belonged to the Arden family who owned the farmstead. Similarly it was decided to use the barns and outbuildings at the rear of the farmhouse as a setting for the display of old· farming implements and other reminders of local community life.

In forty years a considerable collection of items illustrative of farming and rural life and originating for the most part from an area within a radius of twenty miles, has been built up, partly by purchase but chiefly by gift, with the result that the folk-life museum at Mary Arden's House has now become a feature of special interest and importance.

The collection is infinitely varied in its scope but in general comprises all kinds of implements and tools of husbandry, utensils and domestic articles formerly to be found in farms and cottages, together with items illustrative of other aspects of country life such as crafts, communications, sport and pastimes. Some of the bygones are very old, going back as far as Shakespeare's time; others are of more recent date. Nevertheless, they have one characteristic in common in that they provide a physical link with the life of the folk who have peopled the Warwickshire countryside in successive generations.

Tools and implements have been collected to illustrate every process of husbandry in the pre-mechanised world of farming in previous centuries. Among these are examples of the early types of man-propelled breast ploughs, with their later improvements, as exemplified in a variety of wooden and iron horse-drawn ploughs made by local blacksmiths and wheelwrights (*illustrated on pages 124–5*). This particular category includes the last two Warwickshire ploughs made by Troth of Langley. There are also a number of original Warwickshire drills of various patterns, as well as early chaff and root-cutting machines.

Tools now rarely used, such as dibbers for planting beans in the fields and a hopper for sowing seeds, sickles, flails for threshing, straw-band twisters, thatching tools and shepherds' crooks are represented, together with various types of spades, forks, scythes, rakes and harvesting tackle. All these items reflect the skill of the country craftsmen who made them. It is fitting, therefore, that the collection should also include specimens of the tools of the wheelwright, blacksmith, carpenter, cooper and brickmaker, as well as those used by the saddler, shoemaker and glover. One of the larger exhibits set up in the barns is a lathe, operated by a large wooden wheel, which formerly supplied the motive power in a local workshop (*see page 127*).

The stable at Mary Arden's House contains everything to do with horses. Here may be seen examples of different types of harness and gear designed for different purposes, a range of saddlery and carriage accessories, bellows and shoeing tools used by the village blacksmith, and old veterinary instruments. The number and variety of items emphasise the indispensable role played by the horse on farms over the centuries. Even the wooden, manually propelled fire-engine which was formerly used for fighting fires in Stratford and the neighbouring countryside was horse-drawn. This appliance recalls the constant risk of fire in barns and rickyards where the crops were harvested and stored. Fire fighting was rendered all the more difficult in the absence of a main water supply. Like most farms Mary Arden's House relied on a pump and wells for drinking water, while the pond at the back of the barns provided a reserve for general purposes.

Staddle-stones now recall that the area nearby served as the rickyard, and hovels now accommodate representative farm carts and wagons (including a particularly fine example of a Warwickshire wain made in Stratford), together with two types of gypsy caravans, formerly to be seen in the surrounding countryside.

The farmhouse itself is furnished and equipped in a manner designed to give an impression of the practical details of domestic life in the country. Old-time dairy methods are illustrated by a number of churns, pails, cheese and butter-making utensils. The old cider mill preserved in one of the outbuildings recalls the country practice of cider making, while the rectangular stone dovecote or pigeon house, with its 657 nesting-holes built inside the walls, suggests that pigeons were kept for utilitarian and not just prestige purposes.

Country sports and pastimes are recalled by a set of loggats, the quaint instruments of a village band, a variety of firearms, fishing tackle and mantraps at one time used by the gentry to preserve their game. These are shown in the illustration above, together with the stocks – another grim reminder of an earlier method of punishment – a 'boneshaker' bicycle hanging from the rafters and a curious early tricycle.

The 1964 Shakespeare Anniversary

The 400th anniversary of Shakespeare's birth, celebrated in 1964, had a far wider international recognition and significance than the tercentenary celebrations of 1864. Specially bound editions of the plays, translations, books both scholarly and popular, commemorative issues of periodical literature and press features appeared in profusion. Special productions and projects, festivals and exhibitions, not to mention postage-stamps – for the first time in the history of the British postage-stamp another head (that of Shakespeare) appeared alongside that of the reigning sovereign – medals and souvenirs of all kinds brought home to the people of many countries the incalculable enrichment of our common civilisation made by the poetic genius of one man. The 1964 Shakespeare Anniversary Council sponsored china and glass commemorative pieces manufactured by the firms of Wedgwood, Royal Doulton and Webbs English Crystal. New fabrics inspired by Shakespeare and the Warwickshire countryside were made by Tibor and the Birthplace Trust commissioned Paul Vincze to design the official 1964 commemorative medal (*below*).

The Birthplace Trust possesses all the records of the 1964 Shakespeare Anniversary Council which organised the celebrations in Stratford-upon-Avon and co-ordinated similar commemorative activities in this country and abroad. Every event which took place in Stratford is documented. At the same time every possible item relating to the anniversary year, whether from this country or abroad, has been collected, with the result that the Trust probably has the most complete archive of the 400th anniversary year in existence.

Dr Levi Fox showing H.M. Queen Elizabeth The Queen Mother the First Folio of Shakespeare's plays in the library of the Centre on the occasion of her visit in 1964.

Illustrations

SHAKESPEARE FOLIOS

The First Folio edition of Shakespeare's plays published in 1623 was edited by the poet's friends and fellow actors, John Heminge and Henry Condell, and printed by Isaac Jaggard. The preliminary matter includes the title-page incorporating the portrait engraved by Martin Droeshout, the verses of eulogy by Ben Jonson, a list of actors, and a catalogue or contents listing the thirty-six plays.

There are three copies (one perfect) of the First Folio in the Shakespeare Centre library, together with copies of the Second, Third and Fourth Folios issued in 1632, 1663 and 1685.

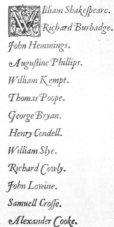

The Workes of William Shakespeare, containing all his Comedies, Histories, and Tragedies: Truely set forth, according to their first ORIGINALL.

The Names of the Principall Actors in all these Playes.

William Shakespeare.	Samuel Gilburne.
Richard Burbadge.	Robert Armin.
John Hemmings.	William Ostler.
Augustine Phillips.	Nathan Field.
William Kempt.	John Underwood.
Thomas Poope.	Nicholas Tooley.
George Bryan.	William Ecclestone.
Henry Condell.	Joseph Taylor.
William Slye.	Robert Benfield.
Richard Cowly.	Robert Goughe.
John Lowine.	Richard Robinson.
Samuell Crosse.	John Shancke.
Alexander Cooke.	John Rice.

FINIS.

Printed at the Charges of W. Jaggard, Ed. Blount, I. Smithweeke, and W. Aspley. 1623.

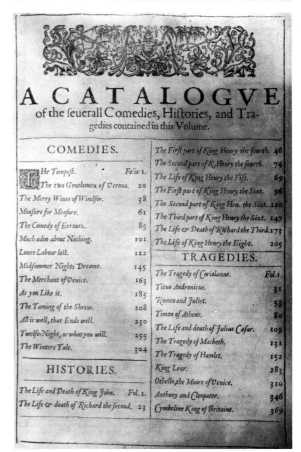

A CATALOGVE
of the seuerall Comedies, Histories, and Tragedies contained in this Volume.

COMEDIES.

The Tempest.	Folio 1.
The two Gentlemen of Verona.	20
The Merry Wiues of Windsor.	38
Measure for Measure.	61
The Comedy of Errours.	85
Much adoo about Nothing.	101
Loues Labour lost.	122
Midsommer Nights Dreame.	145
The Merchant of Venice.	163
As you Like it.	185
The Taming of the Shrew.	208
All is well, that Ends well.	230
Twelfe-Night, or what you will.	255
The Winters Tale.	304

HISTORIES.

The Life and Death of King John.	Fol. 1.
The Life & death of Richard the second.	23
The First part of King Henry the fourth.	46
The Second part of K. Henry the fourth.	74
The Life of King Henry the Fift.	69
The First part of King Henry the Sixt.	96
The Second part of King Hen. the Sixt.	120
The Third part of King Henry the Sixt.	147
The Life & Death of Richard the Third.	173
The Life of King Henry the Eight.	205

TRAGEDIES.

The Tragedy of Coriolanus.	Fol. 1.
Titus Andronicus.	31
Romeo and Juliet.	53
Timon of Athens.	80
The Life and death of Julius Cæsar.	109
The Tragedy of Macbeth.	131
The Tragedy of Hamlet.	152
King Lear.	283
Othello, the Moore of Venice.	310
Anthony and Cleopater.	346
Cymbeline King of Britaine.	369

Mr. WILLIAM
SHAKESPEARES
COMEDIES,
HISTORIES, &
TRAGEDIES.

Published according to the True Originall Copies.

London
Printed by Isaac Iaggard, and Ed. Blount. 1623.

THE
EXCELLENT
History of the Mer-
chant of Venice.

With the extreme cruelty of *Shylocke*
the Iew towards the saide Merchant, in cutting a iust pound of his flesh. And the obtaining
of *Portia*, by the choyse of
three Caskets.

Written by W. SHAKESPEARE.

Printed by *J. Roberts*, 1600.

Of the plays published in separate form as Quartos the collection includes an interesting and important group of which specimens are illustrated here. The date 1600 as shown in *The Merchant of Venice* and *A Midsummer Night's Dream* has been proved to be fictitious and should be 1619. Illustrated opposite also is a single leaf of the second edition of Shakespeare's first publication, *Venus and Adonis*, printed by Richard Field, a Stratfordian who was the son of Henry Field, the Tanner, who was a neighbour of Shakespeare's father.

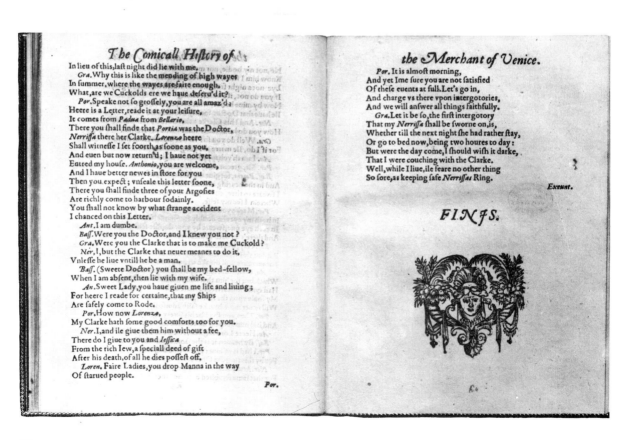

A

Moſt pleaſant and ex-
cellent conceited Comedy,
*of Sir Iohn Falſtaffe, and the
merry VViues of VVindſor.*

VVith the ſwaggering vaine of Ancient *Piſtoll,* and Corporall *Nym.*

Written by W. SHAKESPEARE.

Printed for *Arthur Iohnſon,* 1619.

A

Midſommer nights
dreame.

As it hath beene ſundry times pub-
likely acted, by the Right Honourable, the Lord Chamberlaine his
ſeruants.

VVritten by VVilliam Shakeſpeare.

Printed by Iames Roberts, 1600.

Loues Labours loſt. 6

A WITTIE AND
PLEASANT
COMEDIE,

As it was Acted by his Maieſties Seruants at
the Blacke-Friers and the Globe.

Written

By WILLIAM SHAKESPEARE.

9

LONDON,

Printed by *W.S.* for *Iohn Smethwicke,* and are to be
ſold at his Shop in Saint *Dunſtones* Church-
yard vnder the Diall.

VENVS AND ADONIS.

Hard fauourd tyrant, ugly, meagre, leane,
Hatefull diuorce of loue, (thus chides ſhe death)
Grim-grinning ghoſt, earths-worme what doſt thou
To ſtifle beautie, and to ſteale his breath? (meane?
VVho when he liu'd, his breath and beautie ſet
Gloſſe on the roſe, ſmell to the violet.

If he be dead, ô no, it cannot be,
Seeing his beautie, thou ſhouldſt ſtrike at it,
Oh yes, it may, thou haſt no eyes to ſee,
But hatefully at randon doeſt thou hit,
Thy marke is feeble age, but thy falſe dart,
Miſtakes that aime, and cleaues an infants hart.

Hadſt thou but bid beware, then he had ſpoke,
And hearing him, thy power had loſt his power,
The deſtinies will curſe thee for this ſtroke,
They bid thee crop a weed, thou pluckſt a flower,
Loues golden arrow at him ſhould haue fled,
And not deaths ebon dart to ſtrike him dead.

Doeſt thou drink tears, that thou prouok'ſt ſuch wee-
VVhat may a heauie grone aduantage thee? (ping,
VVhy haſt thou caſt into eternall ſleeping,
Thoſe eyes that taught all other eyes to ſee?
Now nature cares not for thy mortall vigour,
Since her beſt worke is ruin'd with thy rigour.

Here

SHAKESPEARE EDITIONS

THE

WORKS

OF

Mr. *William Shakespear*;

IN

SIX VOLUMES.

ADORN'D with CUTS.

Revis'd and Corrected, with an Account of
the Life and Writings of the Author.
By *N. ROWE*, Efq;

LONDON:

Printed for *Jacob Tonfon*, within *Grays-Inn*
Gate, next *Grays-Inn* Lane. MDCCIX.

Editions of Shakespeare's plays, from the seventeenth century to the present time, constitute a
basic ingredient of the library's collections.
Where originals are not held, facsimile copies
(see the copy of the *Poems* below, which is one
of 250 copies of a reproduction published in
1885) provide adequate substitutes for study purposes. Rowe's edition of 1709 (*left*) initiated a
whole series of versions of editions of
Shakespeare's plays during the eighteenth century. Among modern limited editions represented in the library, the Nonsuch Press edition
(*opposite*), published in 1929, is particularly fine.

This Shadowe is renowned Shakespear's Soule of th'age
The applause: delight! the wonder of the Stage.
Nature her selfe, was proud of his designes
And joy'd to weare the dressing of his lines,
The learned will Confess, his works are such,
As neither man, nor Muse, can prayse to much.
For ever live thy fame, the world to tell,
Thy like, no age, shall ever paralell.

W. M. sculpsit.

POEMS

VVRITTEN

BY

WIL. SHAKE-SPEARE.

Gent.

Printed at *London* by *Tho. Cotes*, and are
to be fold by *Iohn Benfon*, dwelling in
S*t. Dunftans* Church-yard. 1640.

THE TEMPEST

Actus primus, Scena prima.   *(On a ship at sea.)*

A tempestuous noise of Thunder and Lightning heard:
Enter a Ship-master, and a Boteswaine.

Master. Bote-swaine.

Botes. Heere Master: What cheere?

Mast. Good: Speake to th' Mariners: fall too't, yarely, or we run our selves a ground, bestirre, bestirre.   *Exit.*

Enter Mariners.

Botes. Heigh my hearts, cheerely, cheerely my harts: yare, yare: Take in the toppe-sale: Tend to th' Masters whistle: Blow till thou burst thy winde, if roome enough.

Enter Alonso, Sebastian, Anthonio, Ferdinando,
Gonzalo, and others.

Alon. Good Boteswaine have care: where's the Master? Play the men.

Botes. I pray now keepe below.

Anth. Where is the Master, Boson?

Botes. Do you not heare him? you marre our labour, Keepe your Cabines: you do assist the storme.

Gonz. Nay, good be patient.   *good,*

Botes. When the Sea is: hence, what cares these   *hence!* roarers for the name of King? to Cabine; silence: trouble us not.

BOOKS OF SHAKESPEARE'S PERIOD

Numerous books dealing with almost every conceivable kind of subject were published during Shakespeare's lifetime. Some of these, such as *Holinshed's Chronicle*, with its woodcut of the three witches (*right*), provided source material for Shakespeare's plays.

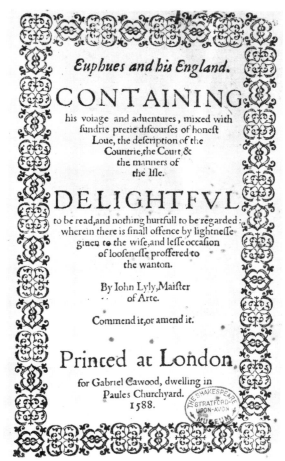

Euphues and his England, first published in 1580

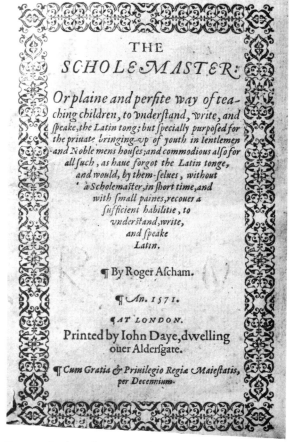

Roger Ascham's practical treatise on education

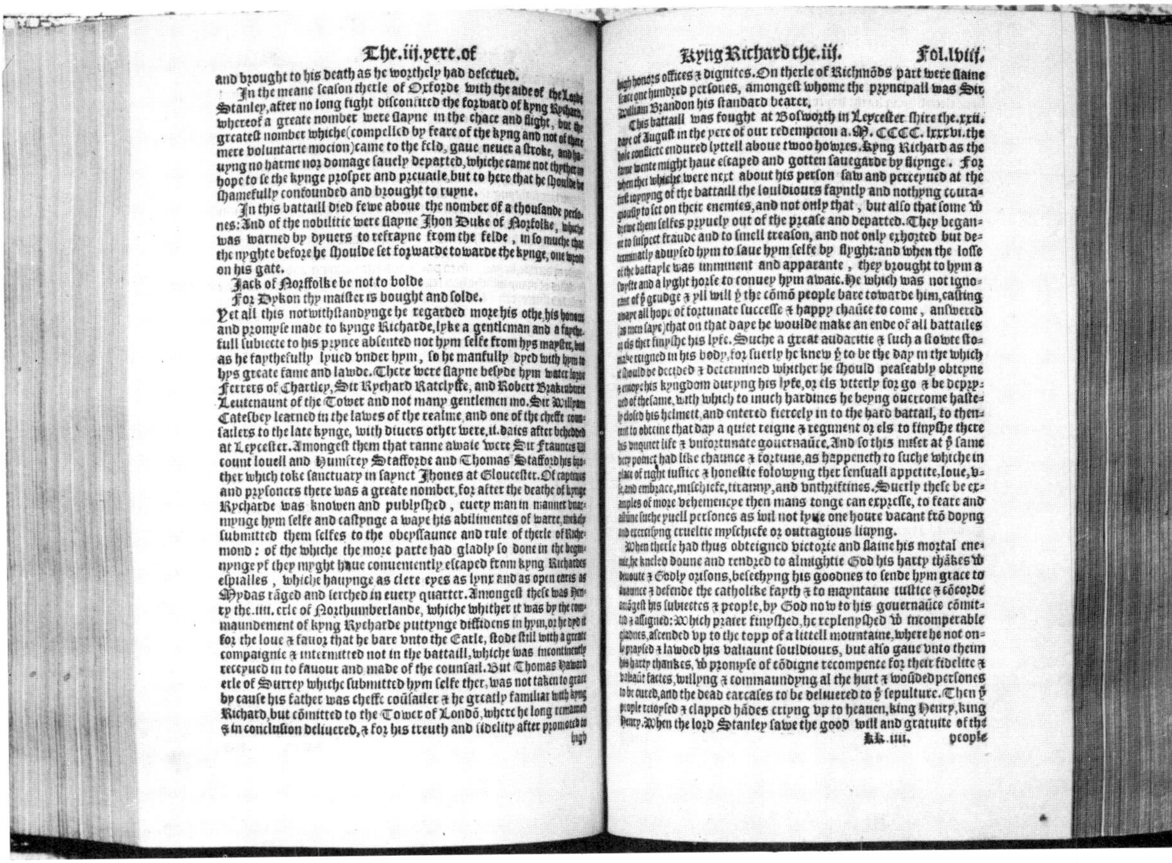

The.iij.yere.of

and brought to his death as he worthely had deserued.

In the meane season therle of Oxforde with the aide of the Lorde Stanley, after no long fight disconfited the forward of kyng Rychard, whereof a greate nomber were slayne in the chace and flight, but the greatest nomber whiche (compelled by feare of the kyng and not of there mere voluntarie mocion) came to the feld, gaue neuer a stroke, and hauyng no harme nor domage sauely departed, whiche came not thyther in hope to se the kynge prosper and preuaile, but to here that he shoulde be shamefully confounded and brought to ruyne.

In this battaill died fewe aboue the nomber of a thousande persones: And of the nobilitie were slayne Jhon Duke of Norfolke, whiche was warned by dyuers to refrayne from the felde, in so muche that the nyghte before he shoulde set forwarde towarde the kynge, one wrote on his gate.

Jack of Norffolke be not to bolde
For Dykon thy maister is bought and solde.

Yet all this notwithstandynge he regarded more his othe, his honour and promyse made to kynge Richarde, lyke a gentleman and a faythefull subiecte to his prynce absented not hym selfe from hys mayster, but as he faythefully lyued vnder hym, so he manfully dyed with hym to hys greate fame and lawde. There were slayne besyde hym water lorde Ferrers of Chartley, Sir Rychard Ratclyffe, and Robert Brakenburie Leutenaunt of the Tower and not many gentlemen mo. Sir Willyam Catesbey learned in the lawes of the realme, and one of the cheffe counsailers to the late kynge, with diuers other were, ii. daies after beheded at Leycester. Amongest them that ranne awaie were Sir Fraunces Vicount louell and Humfrey Staforde and Thomas Staffordhis brother which toke sanctuary in saynct Jhones at Gloucester. Of captiues and prysoners there was a greate nomber, for after the deathe of kynge Rycharde was knowen and publyshed, euery man in manner vnarmynge hym selfe and castynge a waye his abilimentes of warre, mekely submitted them selfes to the obeyssaunce and rule of therle of Richemond: of the whiche the more parte had gladly so done in the begynnynge yf they myght haue conueniently escaped from kyng Richardes espialles, whiche hauynge as clere eyes as lynx and as open eares as Mydas ranged and serched in euery quarter. Amongest these was Henry the.iiii. erle of Northumberlande, whiche whither it was by the commaundement of kyng Rycharde puttynge diffidens in hym, or he dyd it for the loue & fauor that he bare vnto the Earle, stode still with a great compaignie & intermitted not in the battaill, whiche was incontinently receyued in to fauour and made of the counsail. But Thomas Haward erle of Surrey whiche submitted hym selfe ther, was not taken to grace by cause his father was cheffe counsailer & he greatly familiar with kyng Richard, but comitted to the Tower of London, where he long remained & in conclusion deliuered, & for his treuth and fidelity after promoted to high

Kyng Richard the.iij. Fol.lviii.

high honors offices & dignites. On therle of Richmonds part were slaine scant one hundred persones, amongest whome the pryncipall was Sir William Brandon his standard bearer.

This battaill was fought at Bosworth in Leycester shire the.xxii. daye of August in the yere of our redempcion a. M. CCCC. lxxxvi. the hole conflicte endured lyttell aboue twoo howres. Kyng Richard as the fame wente might haue escaped and gotten sauegarde by flyinge. For when thei whiche were next about his person saw and perceyued at the first ioynyng of the battaill the souldiours payntly and nothyng couragiously to set on their enemies, and not only that, but also that some withdrewe them selfes pryuely out of the prease and departed. They began to suspect fraude and to smell treason, and not only exhorted but determinatly aduysed hym to saue hym selfe by flyght: and when the losse of the battayle was imminent and apparante, they brought to hym a swyfte and a lyght horse to conuey hym awaie. He which was not ignorant of the grudge & yll will that the comon people bare towarde him, castyng awaye all hope of fortunate successe & happy chaunce to come, answered (as men saye) that on that daye he woulde make an ende of all battailes or els ther finyshe his lyfe. Suche a great audacitie & such a stowte stomake reigned in his body, for suerly he knew that to be the day in the which it should be decided & determined whither he should peaseably obteyne & enioye his kyngdom durynge his lyfe, or els vtterly forgo & be depryued of the same, with which to much hardines he beyng ouercome hastely closed his helmett, and entered fiercely in to the hard battail, to thentent to obteine that day a quiet reigne & regiment or els to finyshe there his vnquiet life & vnfortunate gouernaunce. And so this miser at the same very poinct had like chaunce & fortune, as happeneth to suche whiche in place of right iustice & honestie folowyng ther sensuall appetite, loue, vse, and embrace, mischiefe, tirannye, and vnthriftines. Suerly these be examples of more vehemencye then mans tonge can expresse, to feare and astonne suche yuell persones as wil not lyue one houre vacant from doyng and exercisyng crueltie myschiefe or outragious liuyng.

When therle had thus obteigned victorie and slaine his mortal enemie, he kneled doune and rendred to almightie God his harty thankes with deuoute & Godly orisons, besechyng his goodnes to sende hym grace to aduaunce & defende the catholike fayth & to mayntaine iustice & concorde amongest his subiectes & people, by God now to his gouernaunce comitted & assigned: Which praier finyshed, he replenyshed with incomparable gladnes, ascended vp to the topp of a littell mountaine, where he not only praysed & lawded his valiaunt souldiours, but also gaue vnto theim his harty thankes, with promyse of condigne recompence for their fidelite & valiaunt factes, willyng & commaundyng al the hurt & wounded persones to be cured, and the dead carcases to be deliuered to the sepulture. Then the people reioysed & clapped handes criyng vp to heauen, king Henry, king Henry. When the lord Stanley sawe the good will and gratuite of the

Kk.iiii. people

A WORLDE of Wordes, Or Most copious, and exact Dictionarie in Italian and English, collected by John Florio.

Printed at London, by Arnold Hatfield for Edw. Blount. 1598

Florio's Italian-English Dictionary, 1598

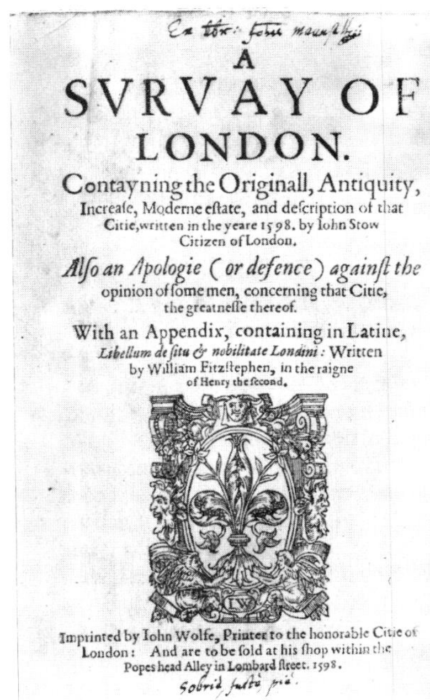

A SVRVAY OF LONDON.
Contayning the Originall, Antiquity, Increase, Moderne estate, and description of that Citie, written in the yeare 1598. by Iohn Stow Citizen of London.

Also an Apologie (or defence) against the opinion of some men, concerning that Citie, the greatnesse thereof.

With an Appendix, containing in Latine, Libellum de situ & nobilitate Londini: Written by William Fitzstephen, in the raigne of Henry the second.

Imprinted by Iohn Wolfe, Printer to the honorable Citie of London: And are to be sold at his shop within the Popes head Alley in Lombard street. 1598.

John Stow's *Survey of London*, 1598

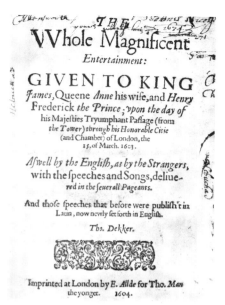

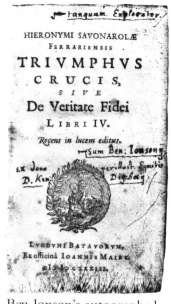

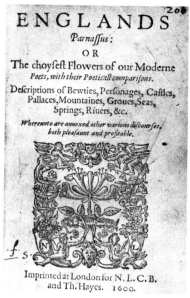

Thomas Dekker's *Entertainment*, 1604 Ben Jonson's autographed copy *England's Parnassus*, 1600

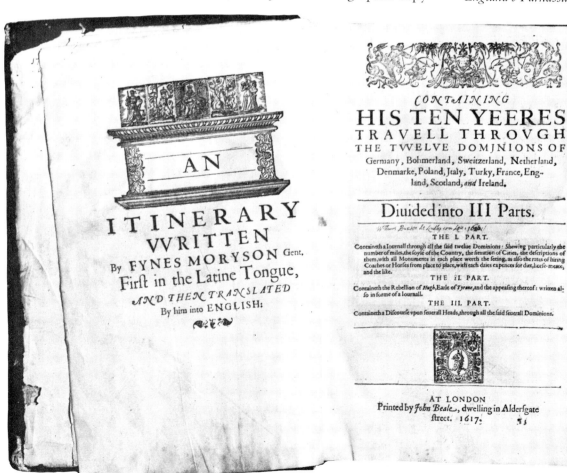

William Burton's copy of Moryson's *Travels*, 1617

Hill's *Gardeners Labyrinth* (1608), a practical handbook on gardening

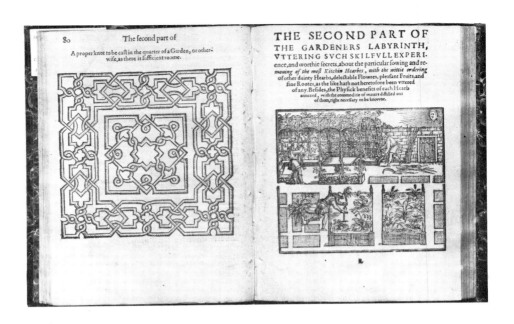

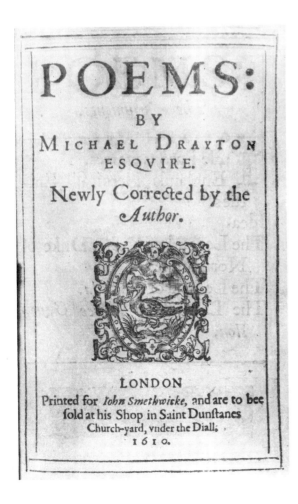

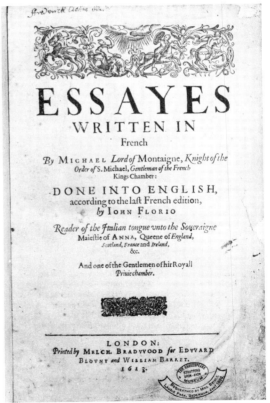

The first English translation of Montaigne's *Essays*, first published in 1603

Poems by Michael Drayton, a Warwickshire friend of Shakespeare

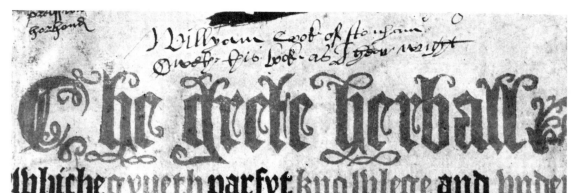

The grete herball

Whiche gyueth parfyt knowlege and vnder
standyng of all maner of herbes & theyr gracyous vertues whiche god hath
ordeyned for our prosperous welfare and helth/for they hele & cure all maner
of dyseases and sekenesses that fall or mysfortune to all maner of creatures
of god created practysed by many expert and wyse maysters (as Auicenna &
other.&c. Also it gyueth parfyte vnderstandynge of the booke lately prynted
by me (Peter treueris) named the noble experiēce of vertuous hand warke of
surgery.

Title-page of the second edition (1529) of *The Great Herbal*, first published in 1526 – a standard treatise on herbs

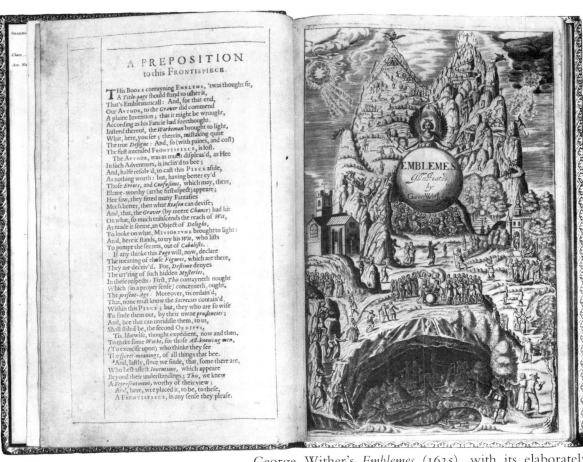

George Wither's *Emblemes* (1635), with its elaborately engraved title-page and separate illustrations of emblems

Ere thou a fruitfull-Cropp ſhalt ſee,
Thy ground muſt plough'd and harro'wd be.

A Princes moſt ennobling Parts,
Are Skill in Armes, and Love to Arts.

DR JOHN HALL

Much is known about the work of Shakespeare's medical son-in-law, Dr John Hall. His case-book, *Select Observations on English Bodies* (1657) (*below*), became a standard handbook for medical students. It gives details of illnesses of some of his patients and the remedies applied. Included are references to Michael Drayton (*right*), and to his own wife, Susanna Shakespeare (*below right*).

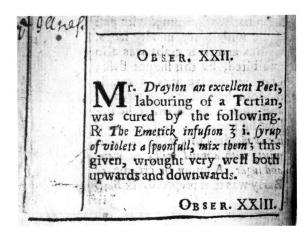

OBSER. XXII.

Mr. *Drayton* an excellent *Poet*, labouring of a *Tertian*, was cured by the following. ℞ *The Emetick infusion* ℥ i. *syrup of violets a spoonfull, mix them*; this given, wrought very well both upwards and downwards.

OBSER. XXIII.

Select Observations ON *ENGLISH* BODIES: OR, Cures both Empericall and Historicall, performed upon very eminent Persons in desperate Diseases.

First, written in Latine by Mr. *John Hall* Physician, living at *Stratford* upon *Avon* in *Warwick-shire*, where he was very famous, as also in the Counties adjacent, as appeares by these Observations drawn out of severall hundreds of his, as choysest.

Now put into English for common benefit by *James Cooke* Practitioner in *Physick* and *Chirurgery.*

London, Printed for *John Sherley*, at the *Golden Pelican*, in *Little-Britain.* 1657.

---

24   *Select Observations*

OBSER. XIX.

Mrs *Hall* of *Stratford* my wife being miserably tormented with the collick, was cured as followeth. ℞ *diaphæn. diacatholic. ana ounce* i. *pul. Holand.* ℥.ii.*ol. Rutæ ounce* i. *Lact. q. s. f Clyst.* this injected gave her two stooles, yet the pain continued being but little mitigated, therefore I appointed to inject a pint of *sack* made *hot*, this presently brought forth a great deale of wind, and freed her from all pain, to her stomack was applyed a plaster *de Labd. Crat. cum Caran. et spec. aromat. rosat. et ol. macis.* with one of these glysters I delivered the *Earle of Northampton* from a grievous collick.

OBSER. XX.

Mrs *Herbert* miserably vexed with a pain of her side, was thus eased; ℞ *Of spirit of wine* or

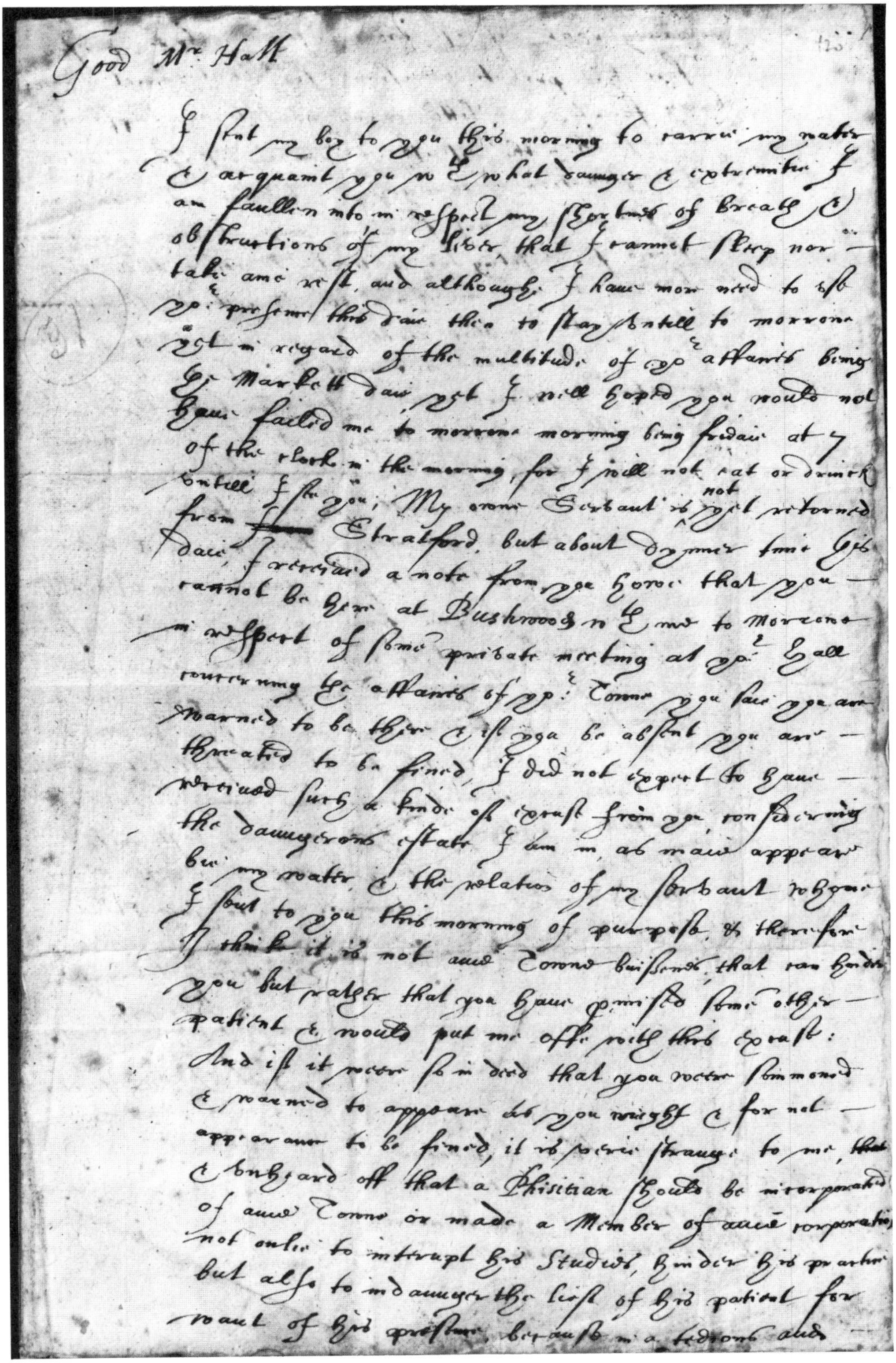
Good Mr Hall

I sent my boy to you this morning to carrie my water
& acquaint you in what danger & extremitie I
am fallen into in respect my shortnes of breath &
obstructions of my liver, that I cannot sleep nor
take anie rest, and although I have more need to use
your presence this daie then to staye untill to morrowe
yet in regard of the multitude of your affaires being
the Markett daie, yet I still hoped you would not
have failed me to morrowe morning being fridaie at 7
of the clock in the morning, for I will not eat or drinck
untill I see you; My owne Servant is not yet returned
from Stratford, but about dynner time this
daie I receiued a note from your horse that you
cannot be here at Bushwood with me to morrowe
in respect of some private meeting at your Hall
concerning the affaires of your Towne you saie you are
warned to be there & if you be absent you are
threatned to be fined, I did not expect to have
receiued such a kinde of excuse from you, considering
the daungerous estate I am in, as maie appeare
bie my water, & the relation of my servant whome
I sent to you this morning of purpose, & therefore
I think it is not anie Towne buisines, that can hinder
you but rather that you have promised some other
patient & would put me off with this excuse:
And if it were so indeed that you were summoned
& warned to appear as you wright & for not
appearance to be fined, it is verie straunge to me, that
& unheard off that a Phisitian should be incorporated
of anie Towne or made a Member of anie corporation
not onlie to interrupt his Studies, hinder his practice
but also to indaunger the liefe of his patient for
want of his presence, because in a tedious and

A unique letter written by a patient to Dr John Hall

The earliest known copy of Shakespeare's will exhibited in the Birthplace

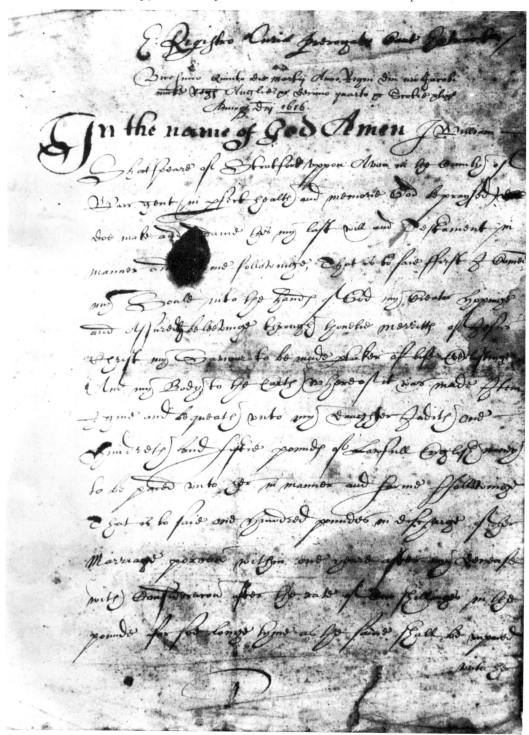

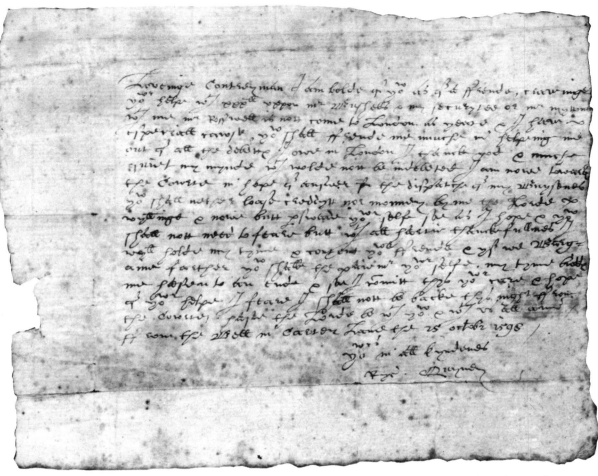

Richard Quyney's letter to Shakespeare asking for a loan of money

The only surviving letter to Shakespeare known to exist

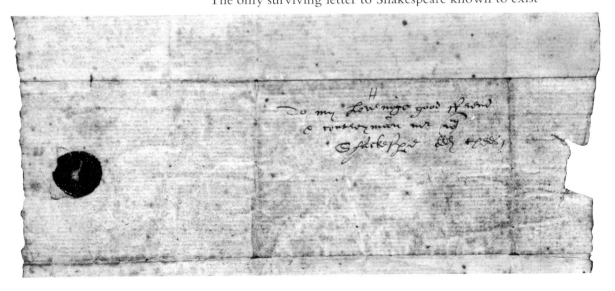

WARWICKSHIRE HISTORY

As an essential reference source alongside its archive collections the Trust's extensive local history library includes both recent publications and the writings of earlier anti-quaries. Warwickshire's first county history by Sir William Dugdale was published in 1656 (*below*). A con-temporary tract records the blowing up of Stratford's Town Hall in 1643 (*opposite top*).

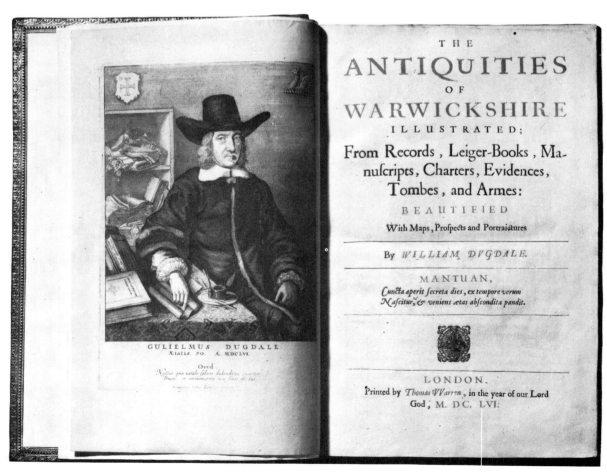

GULIELMUS DUGDALE
Ætatis. 50. A. MDCLVI.

Ovid:
Noster qua natale solum dulcedine cunctos
Ducit et immemores non sinit esse sui.

THE
ANTIQUITIES
OF
WARWICKSHIRE
ILLUSTRATED;

From Records, Leiger-Books, Ma-
nuscripts, Charters, Evidences,
Tombes, and Armes:
BEAUTIFIED
With Maps, Prospects and Portraictures

By *WILLIAM DVGDALE.*

MANTUAN,
Cuncta aperit secreta dies, ex tempore verum
Nascitur, & veniens ætas abscondita pandit.

LONDON,
Printed by *Thomas VVarren*, in the year of our Lord
God, M. DC. LVI.

and the match being lighted, they withdrew themselves from the Hall.

6. *The blowing of the Hall up, and the hurt it did.*

The Lord *Brookes* being marched into the towne of Stratford upon Avon, and taking time to send away the Cavaliers that were taken to VVarwick Gaole, and to settle the towne in quiet, as to cause by strict order that was taken, that none of the army should pillage, or take away any thing from any inhabitants of the towne, which order the souldiers observed with great respect, but by the prolonging of time hereby, it pleased God to preserve the lives of those who live to fight his cause, for which we have all cause to blesse God; for when they thought all had been quiet and well, and the Lord *Brooks*, with the Colonels and Captaines were going to fit in Councell, and at the towne Hall, they heard a noise as if some houses had fallen downe, and looking about they saw the towne Hall, torne in peeces, and a great smoake, which caused a most lamentable and pitifull cry in the towne, and when it was perceived what was done, they went to view this businesse, wherein God had so wonderfully delivered them, and it was found that the Hall was torne in peeces in such a manner that it is utterly ruined, and divers houses thereabouts have received some small damage, one of the townesmen was slaine, and foure more burnt and brused, who are very ill, and this was all the hurt which it did: Oh the great cause that we have to praise God for such

such deliverances as these; the Lord hath done great things for us, if we had but hearts to consider it.

7. *The Lord Brooks his valour before his death.*

The Lord *Brooks* with his Army having rendred great thankes to Almighty God for this great deliverance, for which we have all cause to joyne with them in praising God; he is thereby encouraged to go on for the glory of God, the honour of the King, and good of the Kingdome, being very sensible of Gods goodnesse which he doth apprehend in full measure, and he goes on very nobly with courage and fortitude, and thousands are come, and daily did come to aid him, and were very forward with money, horse and Ammunition according to their power. Neither can I passe by with silence one thing in Mr *Bookers* almanack, for the very next day after Ian. 26. as in his almanack doth appeare, he saith, *Curias civitatum probe perlustravit aut infpexerit, is mira cognoscet,* we have all cause to give God thankes both for this, and all other mercies to poore England, which hath made knowne to us these distracted times.

8. *A relation of the Lord Brooks his death.*

The Lord *Brooks* having with his army marched to Lychfield and there gained the towne with great facility, for the Countrey came in very fast to aid him against the Cavaliers, and having setled the towne (as he thought) his Lordship standing in a window on the street side, was shot through the head by an unfortunate

nate

An account of the Battle of Edgehill, 1642

A History of the Kings of England
by John Rous

The works of Warwickshire and Stratford authors, of which examples are illustrated here, cover a wide range of subject-matter.

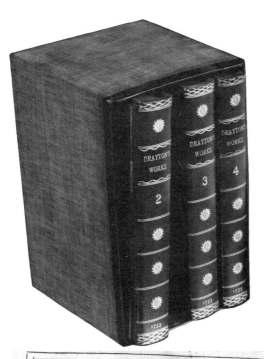

THE
ORNITHOLOGY
OF
FRANCIS WILLUGHBY
OF
Middleton in the County of *Warwick* Esq;
Fellow of the ROYAL SOCIETY.

In Three Books.

Wherein All the

BIRDS

HITHERTO KNOWN,

Being reduced into a METHOD sutable to their Natures, are accurately described.

The Descriptions illustrated by most Elegant Figures, nearly resembling the live BIRDS, Engraven in LXXVIII Copper Plates.

Translated into English, and enlarged with many Additions throughout the whole WORK.

To which are added,

Three Considerable DISCOURSES,

I. Of the Art of FOWLING : With a Description of several NETS in two large Copper Plates.
II. Of the Ordering of SINGING BIRDS.
III. Of FALCONRY.

BY

JOHN RAY, Fellow of the ROYAL SOCIETY.

Psalm 104. 24.

How manifold are thy works, O Lord ? In wisdom hast thou made them all : The Earth is full of thy riches.

LONDON:

Printed by *A.C.* for *John Martyn,* Printer to the *Royal* Society, at the *Bell* in St. Pauls Church-Yard, MDCLXXVIII.

A
BRIDE-BVSH:
OR,
A DIRECTION FOR
MARRIED PERSONS.

PLAINELY DESCRIBING
THE DVTIES COMMON
to both, and peculiar to each
of them.

BY PERFORMING OF WHICH,
marriage shall prooue a great helpe to such,
as now for want of performing them,
doe find it a little hell.

Compiled and published by WILLIAM WHATELY,
Minister and Preacher of God's Word in Ban-
burie *in* Oxfordshire.

Heb. 13. 4.
*Marriage is honourable among all men, and the bed vnde-
filed: but whoremongers and adulterers God will iudge.*

LONDON,
Imprinted by *Felix Kyngston* for *Thomas Man,* and are
to be sold at his shop in Pater-noster-row, at the
signe of the Talbot, 1619.

WELCOMBE HILLS,

NEAR STRATFORD UPON AVON,

A

POEM,

HISTORICAL AND DESCRIPTIVE;

BY JOHN JORDAN OF STRATFORD, WHEELWRIGHT.

The WEST VIEW of WELCOMBE HILLS.

Publishd 1.st Sept.r 1777 by S. Hooper N.o 25 Ludgate-Hill.

LONDON:

Printed for the AUTHOR, and sold by S. HOOPER, No. 25, Ludgate-Hill: G. KEARSLEY, Fleet-Street; S. LEACROFT, Charing-Cross; J. ROBSON and Co. Bond-Street; and J. KEATING, Stratford upon Avon. 1777.

Dearest Brother

Though I am somewhat of the latest as to y Ceremonial part, in wishing you all possible happiness with your Bride, yet ever since I read of your Marriage in the publick papers, I wanted to communicate to you my most affectionate Congratulation on the Occasion, and have been far from satisfi'd that I have done it no sooner.

I beg you will now receive it as Cordially as I sincerely offer it; And as I am fully perswaded you have made a discreet & good Choice, I hope you will prevail with my new Sister to think I have her felicity at heart jointly with Yours, and that You your selves cannot wish it more compleat and permanent than I my self do.

I had been long thinking of a Journey to Coleshill, to pay my respects to Mr Millechamp y Worthy Vicar of that place, for his kindness to my Son; but y long continuance of y Winter, & a Nervous disorder that I have for some time been troubl'd with, quite dishearten'd me from attempting y journey till Easter Monday last, when I set forth from Stratford, intending if the Weather wou'd permit, to have gone on from Coleshill to Lichfield, as I mention'd to Mr Cotton, (partner wth Mr Taylor y Druggist;) but a cold uncomfortable Rain falling on y Wednesday Morning, again dampt my Courage, turn'd my face to Stratford that same day, & prevented my seeing you and Sister Greene as I otherwise wou'd have certainly done. Whether Health & disengagement will permit me that happiness next Whitsun-holidays, is what I cannot yet foresee; My inclination for so doing you may depend upon, not without some hope my Dame will venture to accompany me.

I was yesterday with joy by my Neighbour Mr Morteboys on y Marriage of brother John Greene with Miss Bet. Parsons; who he assured me were link'd in Connubial bands on Wednesday Morning last, & that immediately after y Holy Ceremony was ended, they retir'd to their New Settlement at Kederminster, where being well fixed in their Tabernacle, I wish their Honey-Moon may last as long as such a sweet thing as Honey, and such a bright Planet as the Moon may have their duration.

My Wife joins her Congratulations with mine on your happy Union, & hopes Mrs Greene of Lichfield will not refuse, though from a stranger, y friendly Compliment of her sister Greene of Stratford.

With my love to dear Niece Polly, I ever remain with true esteem

I shall be ever mindful my dear Brother of y extreme kind notice you have taken of my Son; He gloried in it, & I hope he will with me endeavour to make a proper return for it.

Your most affectionate Brother

Joseph Greene

Stratford upon Avon Warwickshire
May y 1st 1762.

The letters, notebooks, drawings and annotated copies of Stratford's antiquaries constitute an invaluable source of local history. *Opposite:* a typical letter of Joseph Greene.
Above: a volume of drawings by Saunders. *Below:* Wheler's annotations

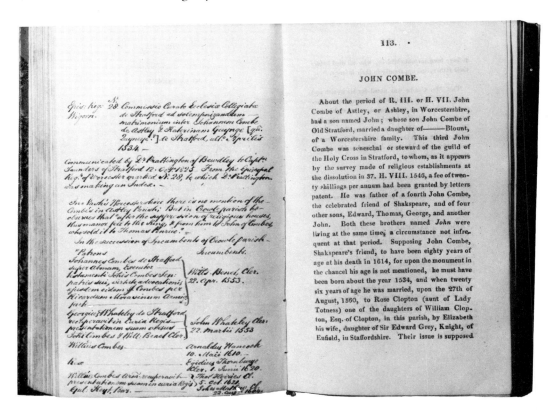

MAPS AND PLANS

Warwickshire and Stratford maps are well represented: Map of Warwickshire, 1610, by John Speed (*right*); the first plan of Stratford, surveyed by Samual Winter in 1759 (*below*).

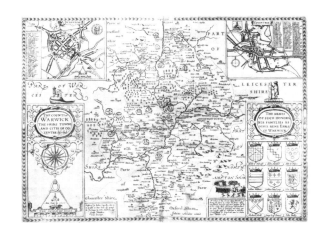

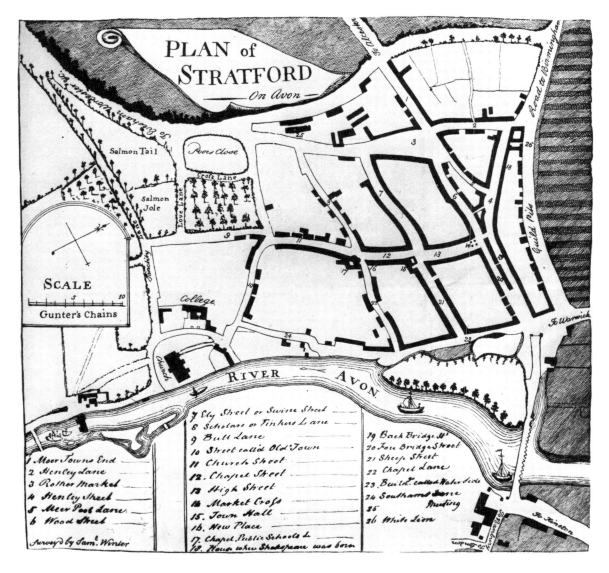

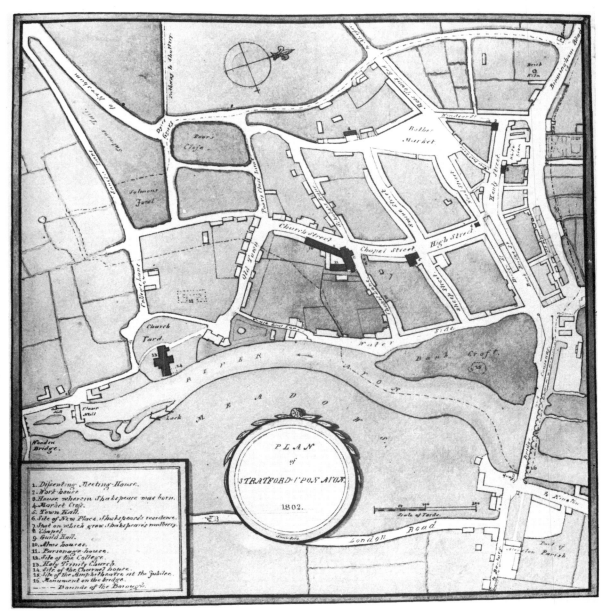

Above: plan of Stratford, drawn by Captain James Saunders in 1802
Left: an allegorical map of Warwickshire which appeared in Michael Drayton's *Poly-Olbion*, published in 1612

Proclamation by James I authorising the inhabitants of Stratford to collect subscriptions from the Midland counties to relieve the town after the fire of 1614.

IAMES, By the Grace of God, King of England, Scotland, Fraunce, & Ireland, Defender of the faith, &c. To all and singuler Archbishops, Bishops, Archdeacons, Deanes, & their Officials, Parsons, Uicars, Curats, and to all spirituall persons: And also to all Justices of Peace, Maiors, Sheriffes, Bayliffes, Constables, Churchwardens, and Headboronghes: And to all Officers, of Citties, Borouhges, and Townes corporate: And to all other our Officers, Ministers, and Subiects whatsoener they bee aswell within Liberties as without, to whome these presents shall come greeting.

WHEREAS wee are credibly certified by a Certificate vnder the hands of our Right trusty and welbeloued Sir Fulke Greuill Knight, Chauncellor of our Exchequer, Sir Thomas Leigh, Sir Edward Deuereux, and Sir Thomas Holt Knights & Barronets, Sir Edward Greuill, Sir Clement Fisher, Sir Clement Throgmorton, Sir Richard Verney, Sir Thomas Lucy, Sir Henry Dymocke, Sir William Somervill, Sir Thomas Beawson, & Sir Henry Rainsford, Knights, Thomas Spencer, Edward Boughton, Bartholomew Hales, Iohn Repington, William Combe,& William Barnes Esquiers, Justices of the Peace within our Counties of Warwicke and Gloucester : That vpon Saturday the Nynetenth day of July last ther happened a suddaine and terrible Fire in our Towne of Stratford vpon Avon within our County of Warwicke, which within the space of lesse then two houres consumed and burnt Fifty and fower dwelling houses, many of them being very faire houses, besides Barnes, stables and other houses of Office, together also with great store of Corne, Hay, Straw, Wood & Timber therein, amounting in all to the value of Eight Thousand Pounds & vpwards, the force of which fire was so great (the wind sitting full vpon the Towne) that it dispersed into so many places therof whereby the whole Towne was in very great daunger to haue bene vtterly consumed & burnt : By reason whereof, and of two seuerall fires happening in the said Towne within these Twenty yeares to the losse of Twenty Thousand Pounds more, not onely our said poore subiects who haue now susteyned this great losse, are vtterly vndone and like to perish, but also the rest of the Towne is in great hazard to be ouerthrowne & vndone, the Inhabitants there being no waies able to relieue their distressed Neighbours in this their great want and misery. And whereas the said Towne hath bene a great Market Towne whereunto great recourse of people was made, by reason of the weekely Market, Faires, and other frequent meetings which were there holden and appointed, and now being thus ruinated & decayed, it is in great hazard to bee vtterly ouerthrowne, if either the resort thither be neglected, or course of trauellers diuerted, which for want of spedy reparation may be occasioned. And so, rasmuch as our said distressed Subiects the Inhabitants of the said Towne are very ready and willing to the vttermost of their powers to redifie & new build the said Towne againe, yet finding the performance thereof farre beyond their ability. They haue made their humble suit vnto vs, that wee would be pleased to prouide some conuenient meanes that the said Towne may be againe redyfied & repaired aswell for the reliefe of the distressed people within the same, as also for the restoring and continuing of the said Market, and haue humbly besought Us, to commend the same good & laudable deed and the charitable furtherance thereof to the beneuolence of all our louing subiects, not doubting but that all good & well disposed Christians wil for common charitie and loue to their Country and the rather for our Commendation heereof be ready with all willingnes to extend their charitable reliefe towards the comfort of so many distressed people, & the spedy performing of so good and charitable a worke.

KNOWE yee therefore, that wee (tendering the lamentable estate and losses of our said distressed Inhabitants, together with the humble suit of all our foresaid Justices made vnto vs on their behalfes) Of our especiall Grace & Princly compassion, haue giue and graunted and by these our Letters Patents doe giue & graunt vnto our welbeloued Subiects William Wyat, Richard Tyler, Isaack Hitchcocke, Richard Mountford, and William Harding, Inhabitants of the said Towne, and to their Deputie & Deputies, the bearer or bearers hereof, full power, licence, & authority, to aske, gather, receiue & take the Almes and charitable beneuolence of all our louing Subiects whatsoeuer inhabiting within our Counties of Warwicke, Leicester, Northampton, Worcester, Gloucester, Oxford, Buckingham, & Berkes, with the Vniuersity of Oxford, & our Cities of Coventry, Peterborough, Worcester, Gloucester, & Bristoll : And in all other Citties, Townes corporate, priuiledged places, Parishes, villages, and in all other places whatsoeuer within our said Counties, & not elsewhere, for, and towards the new building, redyfying, & erecting of the said Towne of Stratford vpon Avon, & the relieuing of all such our poore distressed Subiects their wiues & Children, as haue susteyned losse & decay by the misfortune of the said Fier.

WHEREFORE Wee will and command yov & euery you, that at such time & times as the said William Wyat, Richard Tyler, Isaack Hitchcocke, Richard Mountford, & William Harding, or their Deputie or Deputies, the bearer or bearers hereof, shall come and repaire to any your Churches, Chappels, or other places, to aske and receiue the gratuities & charitable beneuolence of our said Subiects, quietly to permit & suffer them so to do, without any manner your lets or contradictions. And you the said Parsons, Uicars, and Curats, for the better stirring vp of a charitable deuotion, deliberately to publish & declare the Teno of these our Letters Patents vnto our said Subiects, Exhorting & perswading them to extend their liberall contributions in so good & charitable a dad. And you the Churchwardens of euery Parish where such Collection is to be made (as aforesaid) to Collect & gather the Almes & charitable beneuolence of all our louing Subiects, And what shalbe by you so gathered, to endorse on the back-side hereof, and deliuer the same to the bearer or bearers hereof, when as thereunto you shall be required. Any Statute, Lawe, Ordinance, or prouision heretofore made to the contrary in any wise notwithstand.

In Witnes whereof wee haue caused these our Letters to be made Patents for the space of One whole yeare next after the date hereof to endure. Witnes our selfe at Westminster, the First day of December in the Twelueth yeare of our Raigne of England, Fraunce, and Ireland; and of Scotland, the Eight and Fortieth.

Steward.

God saue the King.   *Printed by Thomas Purfoot.*

LOCAL NEWSPAPERS

The files of local newspapers contain unique examples of Stratford's first paper, the *Stratford, Shipston and Alcester Journal*, published between 1750 and 1753.

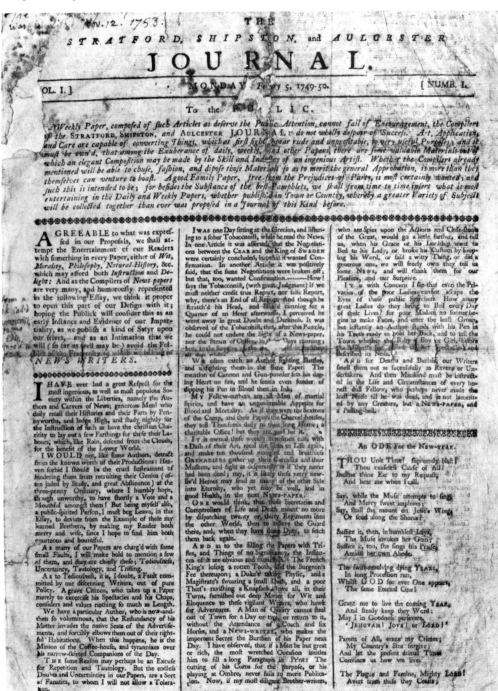

STRATFORD EPHEMERA

Difficult to classify and store but of great interest and value is the vast quantity of miscellaneous material, much of which has been preserved by accident rather than design. It comprises tradesmen's advertisements, sale particulars, broadsides, programmes, reports, election material, invitation cards, book plates, news cuttings, portraits and photographs. Often a single item will throw light on some obscure or unknown aspect of the town's history, its business concerns, local hotels and transport, its roads, bridges and canals, not to mention the recreational side of local community life.

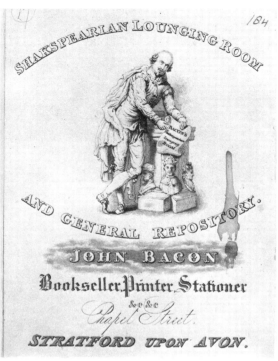

Shakespeare often embellished nineteenth-century advertisements

The Shakespeare Hotel as it originally appeared

Stratford's early coach services

David Garrick stayed at the White Lion Inn in Healey Street (*above*) in 1769

Stratford's Spa at Bishopton, which opened in 1837, never flourished

GARRICK'S JUBILEE

Stratford's first Shakespeare Festival was organised by David Garrick in 1769, the immediate occasion being the dedication of the new Town Hall. Garrick is depicted here (*right*) with the insignia of the office of Steward which he discharged. A fashionable company of ladies and gentlemen took part in a three-day programme of festivities (*opposite*), which included banquets, a masquerade ball and a horse race. The highlight of the Jubilee was Garrick's recitation of the Ode (*below*), which he had composed in honour of Shakespeare.

FIRST DAY,

Wednesday, the 6th of SEPTEMBER,

Shakespeare's Jubilee.

The STEWARD of the JUBILEE begs Leave to inform the COMPANY, that at Nine o'Clock will be

A PUBLIC BREAKFAST

At the TOWN-HALL:

Thence to proceed to the CHURCH to hear

The ORATORIO of JUDITH,

Which will begin exactly at ELEVEN.

From Church will be a full CHORUS of VOCAL and INSTRUMENTAL MUSIC to the AMPHITHEATRE; where, at Three o'Clock, will be

An ORDINARY for Gentlemen and Ladies.

About Five o'Clock, a Collection of NEW SONGS, BALLADS, ROUNDELAYS, CATCHES, GLEES, &c. will be performed in the AMPHITHEATRE; after which the Company is desired to prepare for the BALL, which will begin exactly at Nine, with NEW MINUETS, (composed for the Occasion) and played by the whole Band.

The SECOND DAY's ENTERTAINMENTS will be published To-morrow.

N. B. As the PUBLIC BREAKFASTS and ORDINARIES are intended for those Ladies and Gentlemen who have taken the Guinea Tickets, no Person can be admitted without first shewing such Ticket. Should there be Room for more than the Proprietors of those Tickets, Ladies and Gentlemen will be admitted to the ORATORIO and FIREWORKS, at *Five Shillings* each; and to the DEDICATION, ODE, and BALL, at *Half a Guinea* each.

** The STEWARD hopes that the Admirers of *Shakespeare*, will, upon this Occasion, wear the Favors which are called the *Shakespeare Favors*.

☞ As many Ladies have complained of the Fatigue they shall undergo, if the Ball and Masquerade are on two successive Nights, there will be only the FIREWORKS on *Thursday* Night, and the MASQUERADE on *Friday* Night, the 8th Inst. which will conclude the Entertainments of the Jubilee.

STRATFORD: Printed by FULK WEALE, next Door to the Coffee-House.

Items illustrative of all aspects of the Garrick Jubilee are preserved

THE CELEBRATED GARRICK JUBILEE AT STRATFORD-ON-AVON, IN THE YEAR 1769.

SWEET WILLY

Set by Mr Dibden

The Pride of all Nature was sweet Willy Ho, The Pride of all Nature was sweet Willy Ho, the First of all Swains He Gladd'en'd the Plains, none ever was like to the sweet Willy Ho, the First of all Swains He Gladd'en'd the Plains none ever was like to the sweet Willy Ho, none ever was like to the sweet Willy Ho.

2
He sung it so rarely did sweet Willy O:
He melted each Maid,
So skillfull he Play'd,
No Shepherd e'er Pip'd like the sweet Willy O.

3
All Nature obey'd him the sweet Willy O;
Wherever he came,
What e'er had a Name,
Whenever he sung follow'd sweet Willy O.

4
He would be a Soldier, the sweet Willy O;
When arm'd in the Feild,
With Sword and with Sheild,
The Laurel was won by the sweet Willy O.

5
He charm'd them when living, the sweet Willy O;
And when Willy dy'd,
'Twas Nature that sigh'd
To Part with her All in her sweet Willy O.

LONDON, Printed by John Johnston, at No 11, York street, Covent Garden.

PLAYBILLS

The Stratford-upon-Avon playbills date from the 1760's and comprise Shakespearian and non-Shakespearian bills predating the opening of the Shakespeare Memorial Theatre in 1879, together with those for the Shakespeare Memorial, now the Royal Shakespeare Theatre. The latter group forms an almost complete sequence from the days of Benson through the Bridges-Adams era and the early years of the present theatre opened in 1932, down to the current internationally famous productions. The collection also contains Shakespearian and general playbills both for London and provincial theatres from the eighteenth century to the present. Foreign bills are also represented.

Shakespeare

MEMORIAL THEATRE,

STRATFORD-ON-AVON.

INAUGURAL FESTIVAL

ON

SHAKESPEARE'S BIRTHDAY, WEDNESDAY, APRIL 23, 1879,

AND FOLLOWING DAYS.

WEDNESDAY EVENING, APRIL 23rd,

MUCH ADO ABOUT NOTHING

On this occasion, the Council have the honour to announce that **Mrs. THEODORE MARTIN (HELEN FAUCIT)** has most kindly consented to appear.

Benedick	Mr. BARRY SULLIVAN
Don Pedro	Mr. LUIGI LABLACHE
Don John	Mr. HERBERT JENNER
Claudio	Mr. EDWARD COMPTON
Leonato	Mr. RYDER
Balthazar	Mr. W. H. CUMMINGS
	Who will Sing, "Sigh no more, Ladies,"
Dogberry	Mr. W. H. STEPHENS
Verges	Mr. FRANK BARSBY
Beatrice	Mrs. THEODORE MARTIN (HELEN FAUCIT)
Hero	Miss WALLIS
Ursula	Miss HUDSPETH
Margaret	Miss GOLIEN

Previous to the Performance, **A DEDICATORY ADDRESS**, written by Dr. WESTLAND MARSTON, will be recited by Miss KATE FIELD.

THURSDAY EVENING, APRIL 24th,

HAMLET

Hamlet	Mr. BARRY SULLIVAN
Claudius	Mr. HERBERT JENNER
Polonius	Mr. W. H. STEPHENS
Laertes	Mr. EDWARD COMPTON
Horatio	Mr. LUIGI LABLACHE
Ghost	Mr. RYDER
First Gravedigger	Mr. FRANK BARSBY
Gertrude	Mrs. CHARLES CALVERT
Ophelia	Miss WALLIS
Actress	Miss EMMERSON

FRIDAY EVENING, APRIL 25th,

A CONCERT

The Music of which is associated with the Works of Shakespeare.

Madame ARABELLA GODDARD, Mrs. OSGOOD, Miss KATE FIELD, Madame ANTOINETTE STERLING, Mr. W. SHAKESPEARE, Mr. W. H. CUMMINGS, and Mr. SANTLEY. The LONDON CONCERT GLEE UNION, under the direction of Mr. FRED WALKER.

Conductor..................SIR JULIUS BENEDICT.

SATURDAY AFTERNOON, APRIL 26th,

HAMLET

Will be repeated.

Hamlet	Mr. BARRY SULLIVAN
Claudius	Mr. HERBERT JENNER
Polonius	Mr. W. H. STEPHENS
Laertes	Mr. EDWARD COMPTON
Horatio	Mr. LUIGI LABLACHE
Ghost	Mr. RYDER
First Gravedigger	Mr. FRANK BARSBY
Gertrude	Mrs. CHARLES CALVERT
Ophelia	Miss WALLIS
Actress	Miss EMMERSON

MONDAY AFTERNOON, APRIL 28th,

Mr. SAMUEL BRANDRAM will Recite

"THE TEMPEST."

The Songs incidental to the Play will be sung by Miss de FONBLANQUE.

On MONDAY EVENING, APRIL 28th, and THURSDAY EVENING, MAY 1st,

MUCH ADO ABOUT NOTHING

Benedick	Mr. BARRY SULLIVAN
Don Pedro	Mr. LUIGI LABLACHE
Don John	Mr. HERBERT JENNER
Claudio	Mr. EDWARD COMPTON
Leonato	Mr. RYDER
Balthazar	Mr. W. H. CUMMINGS
	Who will Sing, "Sigh no more, Ladies,"
Dogberry	Mr. W. H. STEPHENS
Verges	Mr. FRANK BARSBY
Beatrice	Miss WALLIS
Hero	Miss EMMERSON
Ursula	Miss HUDSPETH
Margaret	Miss GOLIEN

On TUESDAY EVENING, APRIL 29th, and FRIDAY EVENING, MAY 2nd,

HAMLET

Hamlet	Mr. BARRY SULLIVAN
Claudius	Mr. HERBERT JENNER
Polonius	Mr. W. H. STEPHENS
Laertes	Mr. EDWARD COMPTON
Horatio	Mr. LUIGI LABLACHE
Ghost	Mr. RYDER
First Gravedigger	Mr. FRANK BARSBY
Gertrude	Mrs. CHARLES CALVERT
Ophelia	Miss WALLIS
Actress	Miss EMMERSON

On WEDNESDAY EVENING APRIL 30th, and SATURDAY AFTERNOON, MAY 3rd,

AS YOU LIKE IT

Jaques	Mr. BARRY SULLIVAN
Duke	Mr. ALLERTON
Banished Duke	Mr. LUIGI LABLACHE
Orlando	Mr. EDWARD COMPTON
Adam	Mr. RYDER
Touchstone	Mr. FRANK BARSBY
Amiens	Mr. W. H. CUMMINGS
	Who will Sing, "Blow, blow, thou Wintry Wind,"
Rosalind	Miss WALLIS
Audry	Miss HUDSPETH
Celia	Miss EMMERSON
Phœbe	Miss GOLIEN

Return Tickets at Reduced Fares.—SPECIAL TRAINS after the Performances to Leamington Every Evening; to Birmingham on 23rd and 24th; and to Worcester on 25th and 28th, stopping at intermediate stations.

For further particulars see Official Programme, to be had Price 6d. on application to the Festival Ticket Office, New Place, Stratford-on-Avon.

All the Evening Performances will begin at 7 o'clock; doors open at 6-15 p.m. Those in the Afternoon begin at 2 o'clock; doors open at 2-15 p.m.

PRICES OF ADMISSION (for Seats Numbered and Reserved):—

WEDNESDAY, April 23rd, 20s., 10s., & 5s. THURSDAY, April 24th, 20s., 10s., 5s., & 2s. 6d. REMAINDER OF FESTIVAL, 10s., 5s., & 2s. 6d.

Remittances for Tickets can be sent by Post, addressed to Mr. E. DOWNING, New Place, Stratford-on-Avon, and the best available places will be selected by the Strangers' Committee.

JAMES UPTON, BASKERVILLE STEAM-PRINTING WORKS, GREAT CHARLES STREET, BIRMINGHAM.

SHAKESPEARE FESTIVALS

Stratford's Shakespeare Festivals, from the Garrick Jubilee of 1769 to the present time, are extremely well documented and the Birthplace collections contain an almost complete archive of them. The local Shakespeare Club, formed in 1824, originated the idea of holding an annual anniversary dinner on the poet's birthday.

SECOND COMMEMORATIVE

FESTIVAL

AT STRATFORD-UPON-AVON,

In honour of the Natal Day of

SHAKSPEARE,

THE KING'S ADOPTED BIRTH DAY,

AND THE FESTIVAL OF ST. GEORGE,

On the 23d of April, 1830, and following Days,

Under the direction of the Shakspearean Club established at the Falcon Inn in the Year 1824.

PATRONS,

THE RIGHT HONOURABLE

THE EARL OF PLYMOUTH, High Steward

Of the Borough of Stratford-upon-Avon—

SIR GRAY SKIPWITH, Bart. Recorder,

WILLIAM HUNT, Esq. Steward of the Court of Record,

AND THE CORPORATION.

"———— Be we the first
That shall salute our Rightful Sovereign
With honour of his Birthright to the Crown."

"———— We will not be slack
To play our part in Shakspeare's Pageant,
And keep our great St. George's Feast withal."

The Members of the Shakspearean Club, in pursuance of Resolutions formed in the year 1827, propose holding their Second Commemorative Festival in honour of the above events, on Friday, Saturday, Monday, and Tuesday, the 23d, 24th, 26th, and 27th Days of April, 1830, on which occasion the following Entertainments will take place.

FIRST DAY.

PAGEANT

Of Shakspeare's principal Dramatic Characters,

PRECEDED BY

St. GEORGE,

On Horseback, in full Armour, attended by his Esquire, will leave Mr. RAYMOND's PAVILION in ROTHER STREET precisely at Eleven o'Clock, and move through the Streets of Stratford in the following order—

THE ROYAL STANDARD OF ENGLAND.

Full Military Band.

ST. GEORGE, ON HORSEBACK, IN FULL ARMOUR.

St. GEORGE'S BANNER, BORNE BY HIS ESQUIRE, ON HORSEBACK.

Programme of the ambitious three-day festivities
organised by the Shakespeare Club in 1830

The tercentenary celebrations of 1864, which lasted a week,
included all the traditional pageantry and festival activities

SHAKESPEARE STATUES

As with Shakespeare portraits, so with statues and busts, the Trust's collection includes a considerable number and variety of three-dimensional representations of the poet. The Staffordshire figure below and the pine-wood carving opposite were based on the Shakespeare statue in Westminster Abbey; those on the left are typical busts of the last century.

SHAKESPEARE PORTRAITS

Apart from the bust of Shakespeare by Janssen in Holy Trinity Church, and the engraving by Droeshout in the Folio of 1623 (*see page 39*), both made shortly after the poet's death, a considerable number of Shakespeare portraits have been produced. Among the most important are the Chandos portrait (*right*) in the National Portrait Gallery, the Ely Palace portrait exhibited in Shakespeare's Birthplace (*below*), and George Vertue's engraved portrait of 1719 (*lower right*), Ozias Humphrey's copy of the Chandos portrait, 1783, and the Chesterfield portrait by Zuccara.

The Trust's portrait of Shakespeare by Gerard Soest (d. 1681)

SHAKESPEARIANA

During the eighteenth and nineteenth centuries a large number of attractive Shakespearian souvenirs were produced. Below are shown a selection of Staffordshire potlids depicting Stratford scenes and a fine early nineteenth–century Worcester porcelain jug showing Holy Trinity Church.

Holy Trinity Church

Shakespeare's birthroom

The Birthplace

Anne Hathaway's Cottage

The Shakespeare Club at Stratford was founded in 1824 for the purpose of arranging festivals in the poet's honour and below are some mementoes of its early days. *Left:* cut-glass goblet engraved with a profile bust of Shakespeare and presented to the Club in 1830. *Right:* Staffordshire salt-glaze cider mug of the same period, depicting Shakespeare, his crest, and characters from the plays.

Eighteenth-century casket carved from the wood of Shakespeare's mulberry tree

PICTURES AND PRINTS

Among the Trust's picture collection are a number of portraits of contemporaries of Shakespeare and other notable Stratfordians through the centuries. *Right:* portrait of Joyce Clopton, afterwards Lady Totnes, painted in 1590. *Below right:* Sir George Carew (1555–1624), Baron Carew of Clopton, Earl of Totnes, soldier, politician and antiquary, appointed first High Steward of Stratford in 1610. *Below left:* a portrait by William Dobson of Sir Edward Walker, (1612–77) Garter King at Arms and a keen Royalist supporter during the Civil Wars. In 1675 he purchased New Place, following the death of Lady Barnard, Shakespeare's granddaughter.

Sir Walter Scott before the Shakespeare monument in the chancel of Holy Trinity Church, on the occasion of his visit in 1828. Oil painting attributed to Sir Walter Allen

STRATFORD VIEWS

Although Stratford has retained more of its historic buildings and character than many towns of comparable size, changes have inevitably taken place during the 400 years since Shakespeare's time. It follows that the collections of drawings, prints, and, for more recent times, photographs, assembled by the Trust over a long period are of great value in that they record changes in the town's physical aspect over the years. Indeed, from early representations it is possible to appreciate how Stratford's streets and buildings, some long since demolished, must have appeared to early visitors. Of special interest are the early views of the Shakespearian properties, as, for instance, the Birthplace before restoration when the timberwork of the *Swan and Maidenhead* inn portion was disguised behind a façade of brick; or Nash's House in the late eighteenth century disguised beyond recognition underneath a fashionable Georgian façade.

Stratford's old Market Cross; drawn by Saunders, *c.* 1810

View of the Avon and church in the early 1700's

Chancel of Holy Trinity Church; early nineteenth-century watercolour, artist unknown

Watercolour by Thomas Girtin of the Old Charnel House which until 1800 adjoined the chancel of Holy Trinity Church

The Town Hall, looking down Chapel Street; drawn by Saunders, *c.* 1810

Greenhill Street in 1896; watercolour by E. A. Phipson

Middle Row, Bridge Street, at the turn of the last century; watercolour by Paul Braddon

Henley Street in 1835; watercolour by Celina Flower

Wood Street in 1835; watercolour by Celina Flower

The Gild Chapel from the Grammar School quadrangle; watercolour by F. W. Whitehead, *c.* 1900

Chapel Street at the turn of the last century; watercolour by Paul Braddon

Engraved view from Welcombe, 1830

Barn in Chapel Lane used as a theatre, c. 1805, by Saunders

Mason's Court in Rother Street; from a watercolour by E. A. Phipson, 1896

View of Ely Street from Rother Street; watercolour by E. A. Phipson, 1896

Engraved view of Anne Hathaway's Cottage in 1795

Charlecote House with the Gatehouse; a typical nineteenth-century engraving

Clopton House from an engraving of 1821

Victoria Spa at Bishopton, opened in 1837; from a contemporary lithograph

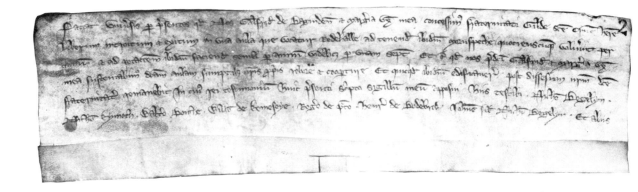

RECORDS OF THE GILD OF THE HOLY CROSS

Stratford's development and prosperity during the Middle Ages owed much to the Gild of the Holy Cross. Founded in the thirteenth century to erect a hospital and oratory, the fraternity came to concern itself not only with spiritual matters – it built the Gild Chapel – but with the provision of educational and welfare services for the local community. The Gild came to own considerable property from which it drew its income, and by the fifteenth century had virtually become the governing body of the town. Its surviving records include deeds – the above document, *c.* 1300 in date, contains the earliest reference to the 'Rodehalle' (Gildhall) – rentals, account rolls and a membership register (*below*) recording the names of the brethren and sisters.

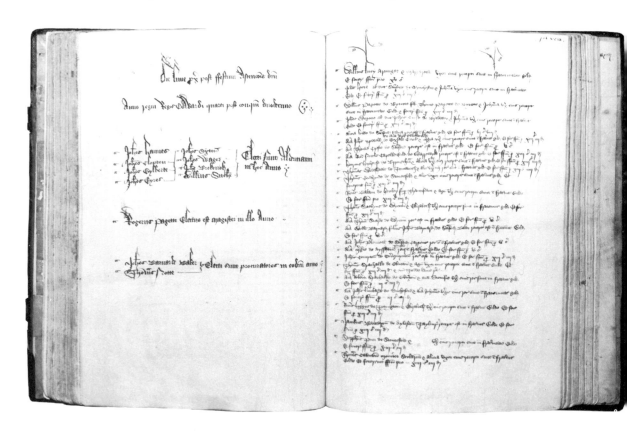

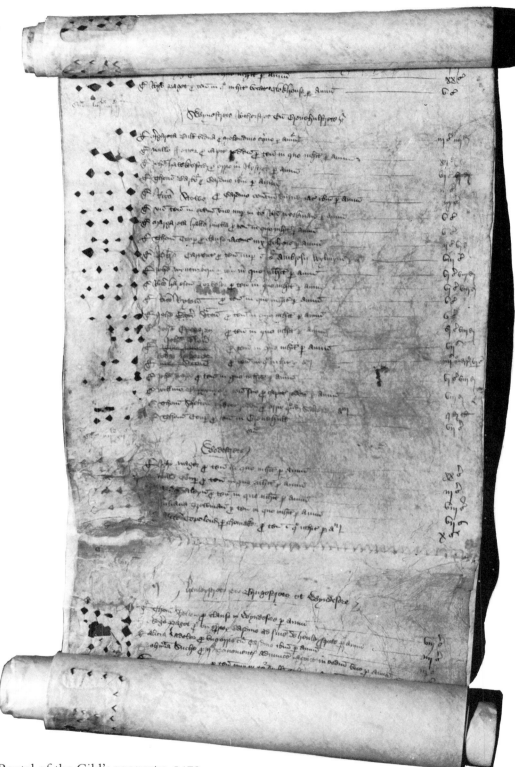

Rental of the Gild's property, 1479

BOROUGH RECORDS

The Borough of Stratford was incorporated by charter in 1553 and an almost complete collection of records relating to the activities of the Corporation from that time has survived. The Borough Records are held on deposit by the Trust. They contribute a unique source for the history of Shakespeare's town.

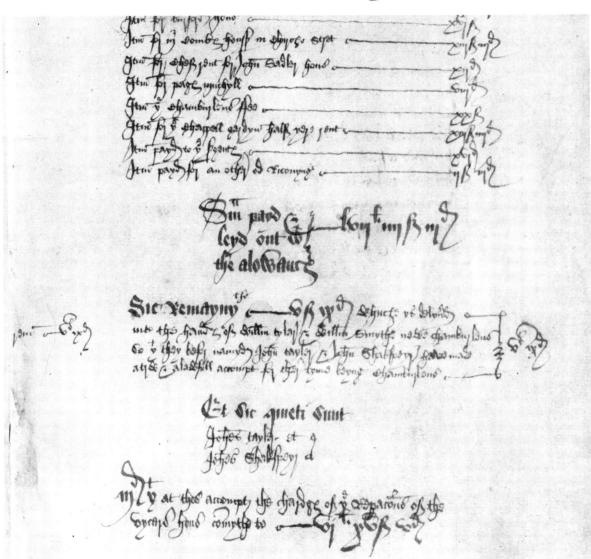

Accounts for 1563–4, when John Shakespeare, the poet's father, was Chamberlain

Minutes of a Council meeting in September 1571, recording John Shakespeare's election as Alderman

Above: Constable's accounts, 1588, and survey of Corporation property, 1582
Below: receipt for repair of Clopton Bridge, 1653

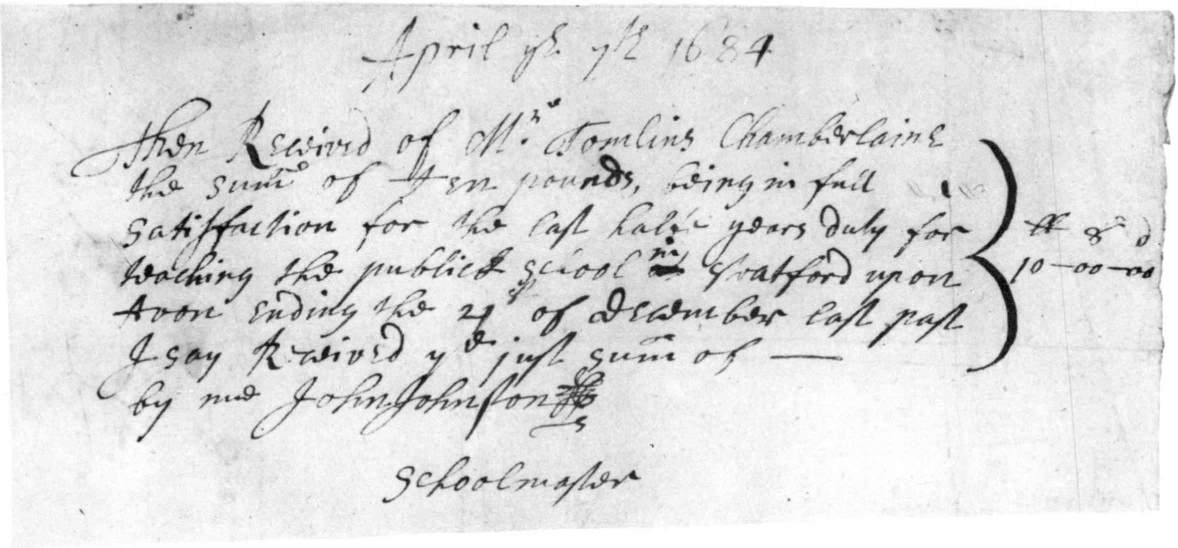

April ye 7th 1684

Then Received of Mr Tomlins Chamberlaine the sum of ten pounds, being in full satisfaction for the last halfe years duty for teaching the publick school in Stratford upon Avon ending the 25th of December last past I say Received ye just sum of — by me John Johnson

Schoolmaster

£ s d
10—00—00

Among numerous bills and vouchers preserved are interesting receipts such as that of John Johnson, headmaster of Stratford's grammar school, for his salary (*above*). Surviving surveys include the Note of Corn and Malt stored in the town in 1598 which enters Shakespeare's name under Chapel Street (*below left*). Toll books recorded the details of horses sold, with the particulars of identification, at Stratford Fairs (*below right*).

143

1602

43

The tolle booke of horses, geldings, mares & coltes, sold or exchanged in the open faire holden in Stratford upon Avon in the Countye of Warwicke the third day of May

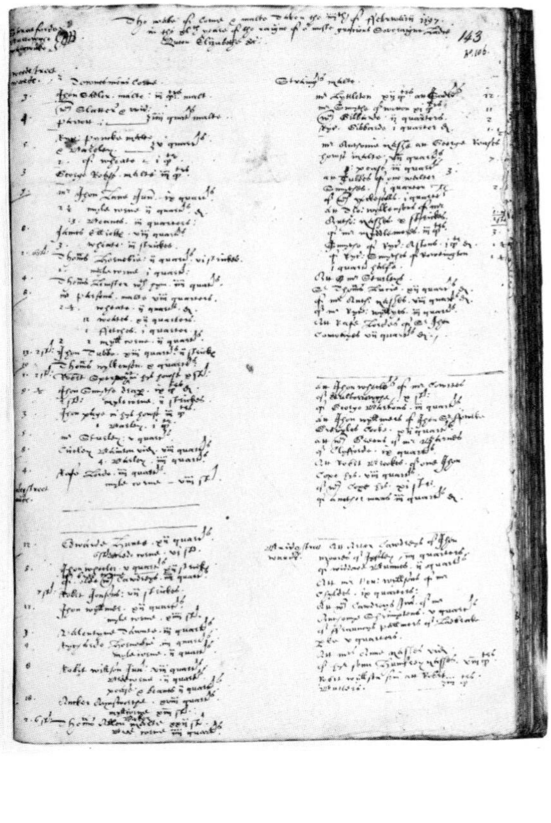

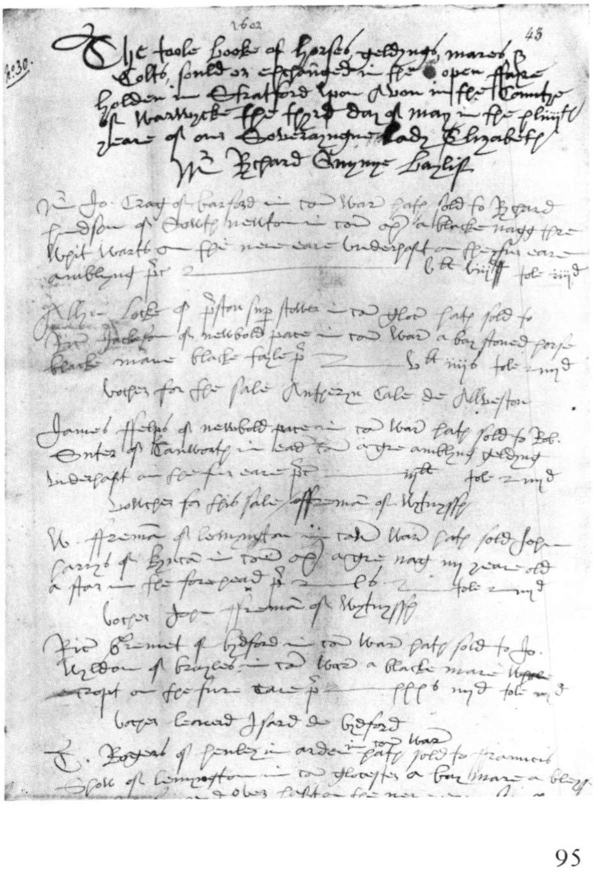

Charter of Hugh, Earl of Chester, granting land in Coventry to
Liulf de Brinklow, *c.* 1177–80 (Gregory-Hood collection)

The Stoneleigh Leger Book, a cartulary compiled by Thomas Pype,
Abbot of Stoneleigh, in the late fourteenth century (Leigh collection)

Henry III's charter to Stoneleigh Abbey, 1227 (Leigh collection)

Charter of Gerard Pucelle, Bishop of Coventry, c. 1183 (Gregory-Hood collection)

Bull of Pope Boniface IX, with lead seal authorising Thomas Archer to choose his own confessor, 1393 (Archer collection)

COURT ROLLS AND ESTATE RECORDS

The family collections deposited with the Trust include a great variety of records which throw light on the administration of landed estates. They comprise court rolls, deeds, rentals, surveys, accounts and business correspondence ranging in date from the twelfth to the twentieth centuries. The court rolls illustrated here relate to the Worcestershire estates of the Throckmorton family of Coughton Court.

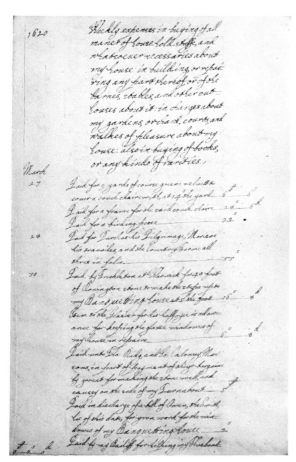

Sir Thomas Puckering's account book, 1620 (Archer collection)

A decorative heading, 1570

Arthur Gregory's register of deeds, *c.* 1580 (Gregory-Hood collection)

Valuation of livestock taken from Lord Leigh's estates during the Civil War (*right*)

PRIVATE RECORDS

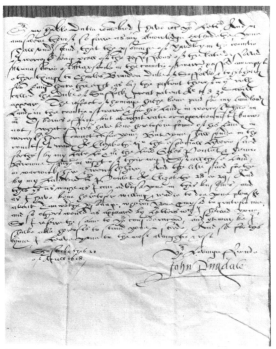

These illustrations typify the infinite variety of private records: *above*, a letter from John Dugdale to Andrew Archer, 1618 (Archer collection), and a haberdasher's bill, 1631 (Leigh collection); *below*, the commonplace book of the dramatist, Sir Francis Fane, d. 1689

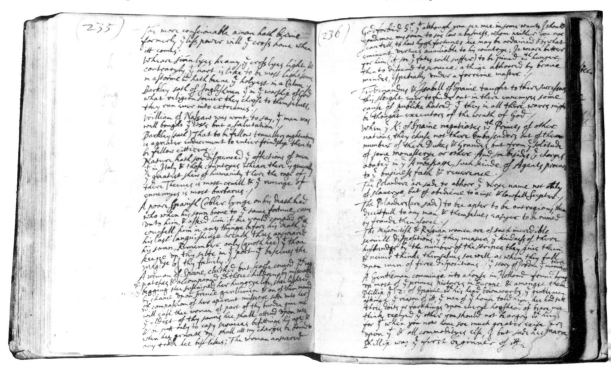

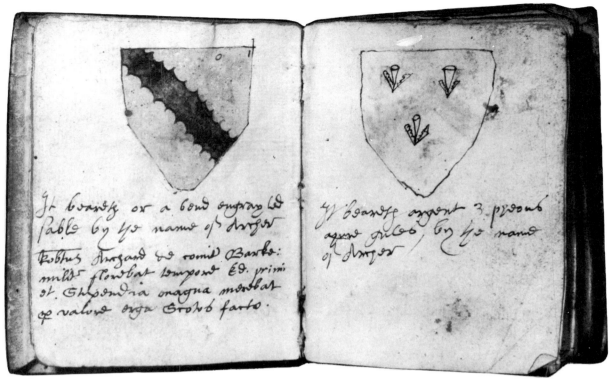

Above, genealogical notes and pedigrees compiled by Sir Simon Archer, antiquary, friend and collaborator of Dugdale (Archer collection); *below*, recipes in a seventeenth–century medical manuscript, known as *Liber Magister Cooke*

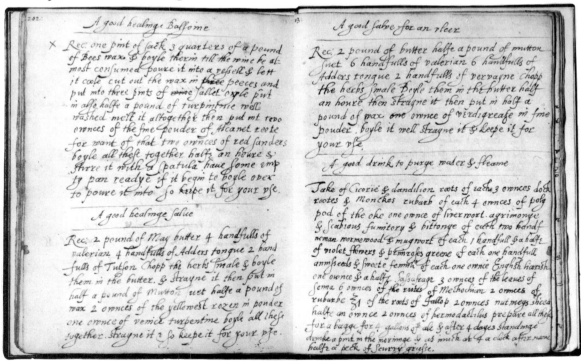

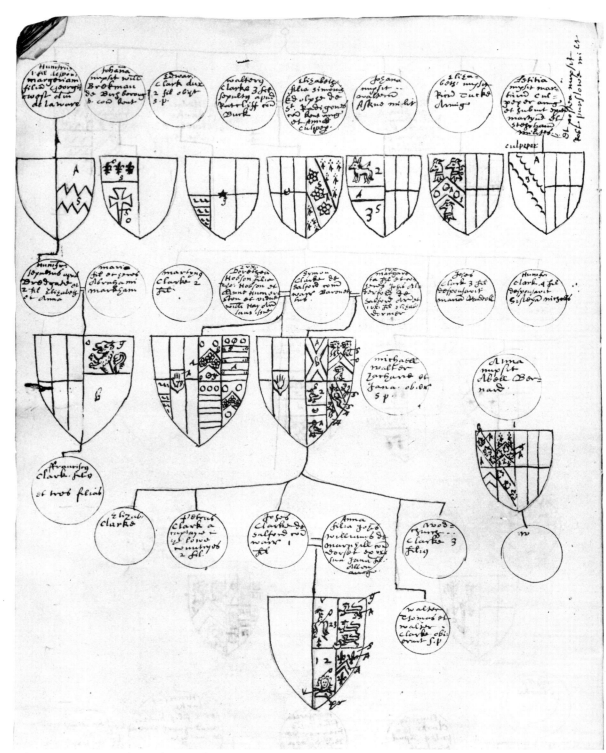

Above: more genealogical notes by Sir Simon Archer (Archer collection)
Opposite: passport granted to Sir Edward Peyto to 'travayle into the parts beyond the seas', 1613 (Willoughby de Broke collection)

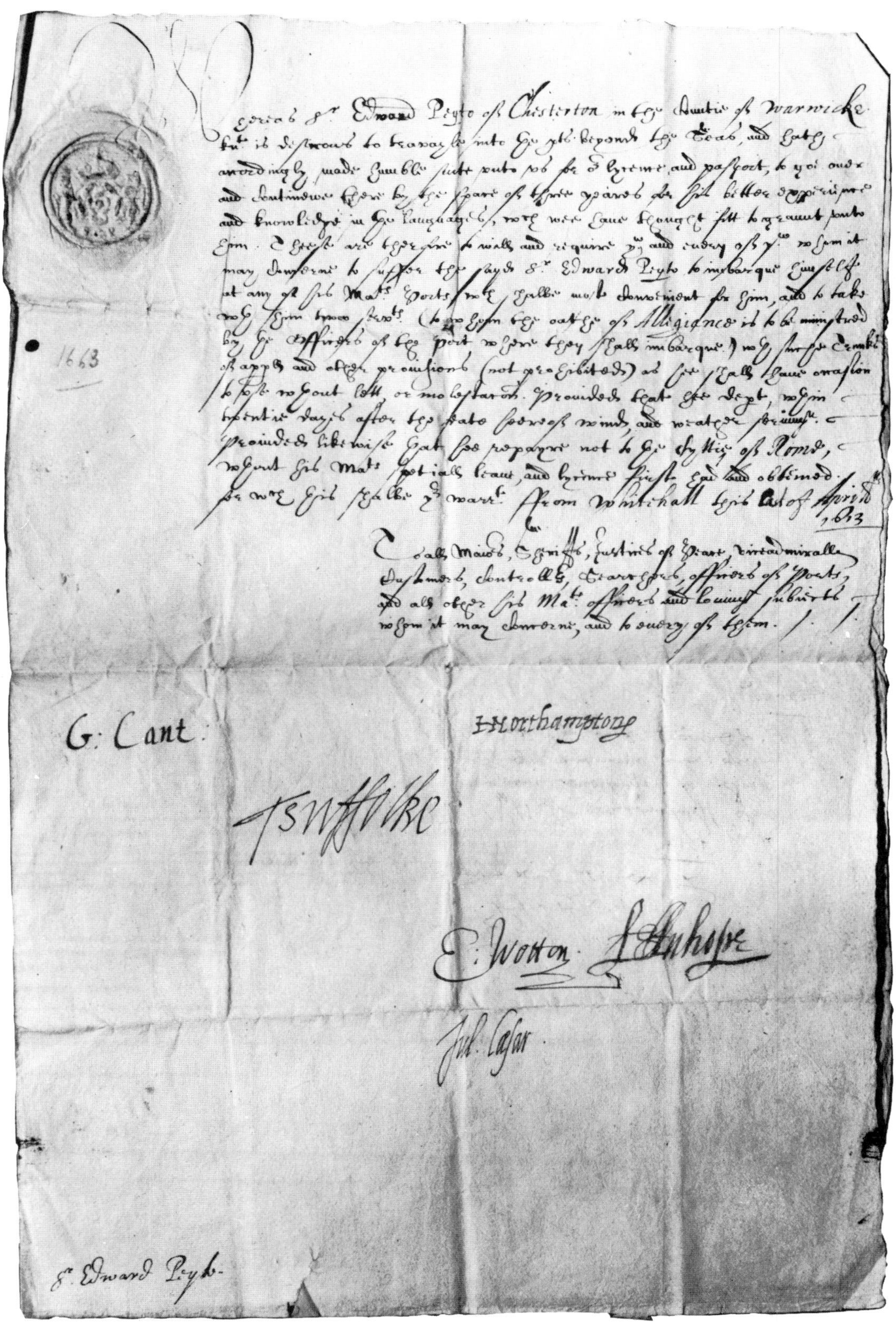

Whereas Sr Edward Peyto of Chesterton in the Countie of Warwicke
Knt is desirous to travayle into the partes beyond the Seas, and hath
accordingly made humble suite unto us for our Lycence and passport, to yor owne
and continuance there by the space of three yeares for his better experience
and knowledge in the Languages, wee wee have thought fitt to graunt unto
him. These are therefore to will and require you and every of you whom it
may concerne to suffer the sayd Sr Edward Peyto to imbarque himselfe
at any of his Mats Portes now shall bee convenient for him, and to take
with him three horses (he haveing the oathe of Allegiance to bee ministred
by the officers of the port where they shall imbarque) wth such other trunckes
of apparell and other provisions (not prohibited) as hee shall have occasion
to take wthout lett or molestacion. Provided that the depte wthin
twentie dayes after the date hereof wind, and weather serving.
Provided likewise that hee repayre not to the Citty of Rome,
wthout his Mats speciall leave, and lycence first to bee obtained.
So wee bid you fare yee well. from Whitehall this of Aprill
1663.

To all Mayors, Sheriffes, Justices of Peace, Viceadmiralls,
Deputies, Constables, Searchers, officers of Portes,
and all other his Mats officers and loveing subiects
whom it may concerne, and to every of them.

G: Cant: Northamptons

        Suffolke

                    E: Wotton L. Chichester

            Jul. Caesar

Sr Edward Peyto

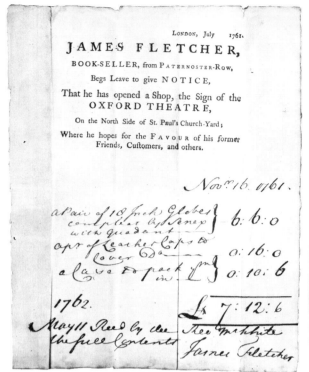

To be SOLD (*Extremely Cheap*)
For *Ready Money* only,
At the QUEEN's HEAD and STAR,
In *Chandos-Street, Covent-Garden*:

A Large and elegant Affortment of the moft Fafhionable SILKS, for the prefent Seafon, confifting of Royal Brocades. Enamel'd, Tobin'd, Spotted, Chevern'd and Strip'd Luteftrings. With great Variety of Tiffues, Vellarets, Peruvians, Flower'd and Water'd Tabbies; Sattins and Plain Silks of every Kind. Likewife a curious Affortment of Black Silks and Bombazeens, very reafonable.

Family collections frequently contain personal and household bills and accounts which throw light in fascinating detail on the social background, tastes and fashions of the period to which they relate. These are three examples of eighteenth-century bills and advertisements from the Leigh collection.

Diary of Robert Hobbes, a Stratford solicitor, for the year 1801

Personal accounts, including winnings and losses at cards,
kept by a young member of the Leigh family in 1764

PREHISTORIC AND
ROMAN ARCHAEOLOGY

Evidence of prehistoric man in the Stratford area is provided by stone and flint implements dating to the Neolithic and Bronze Ages (*right*). In the later Iron Age nearby Meon Hill was fortified and iron currency bars, serving instead of money, were discovered there in the last century (*below*). During Roman times a small settlement developed near the site of Stratford beside the Roman road linking the Fosse with Rycknield Street and excavations have produced quantities of pottery both local and imported (*below left*), iron work manufactured on the site (*top right*) and a fine copper bowl (*below right*)

Decorated Samian bowl (*above*) and coarse-ware drinking beakers
(*below*) from the Roman settlement at Tiddington, Stratford

ANGLO-SAXON ANTIQUITIES

Grave goods, including a decorated drinking
vessel, armlet and combs of bone, bronze applied
brooch, and necklaces of amber, glass and gaily
decorated paste beads, found during excavations
in the sixth-century Saxon cemetery at Stratford.

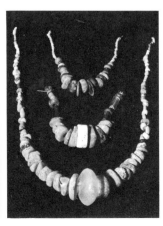

Above: bronze brooches enriched with gold and silver gilt and ornamented with intricate zoomorphic and interlaced patterns

Left: a situla or 'bucket' with bronze bands and iron handle and a bronze workbox from a child's grave

The massive elm chest, carved oak figures and the early maces which belonged to the Gild

DOMESTIC ITEMS

Early wine bottles; a cast-iron pestle and mortar, with a medieval wash-stand and bowl; an ink horn; a rush-light holder

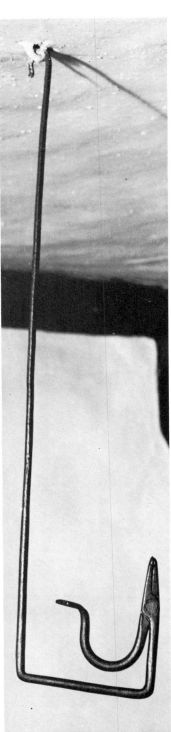

A selection of Elizabethan and Jacobean household utensils, including an early bookbinder's press. The cooking spit at New Place (*right*)

An oak 'baby-minder' of the seventeenth century in the kitchen of Shakespeare's Birthplace

APOTHECARIES' JARS

A late sixteenth-century Venetian apothecary jar with the inscription S D POLIPODIO or 'Syrup of Fern'. The jar is ornately decorated with a design worked in yellow and dark blue surrounding the centrally placed sacred monogram. Each handle terminates in a lion mask

Part of a collection of sixteenth- and seventeenth-
century apothecary jars made in Italy on display
in the dispensary at Hall's Croft

COMMUNITY LIFE

Various items which belong to the Corporation of Stratford illustrating different aspects of local community life in former days are preserved in the Trust's museum collection. *Right:* a standard gallon measure made from copper and dated 1794. *Below:* an early horse-drawn fire engine in the Folk Life Museum at Wilmcote

Other Borough items include standard weights and scales, equipment of the early Borough Police Force and a few pieces of a Staffordshire dinner service bought in 1824

BARCHESTON TAPESTRIES

In the middle of the six-teenth century, at the manor of Barcheston in south Warwickshire, the Sheldon family set up the first 'tapestry factory' in England, an industry that continued there for some ninety years. Most famous of the Barcheston tapestries were the reproductions of maps based on Saxton's *Surveys of the Counties of England*, but biblical and mythological subjects formed the main scenes in most of the tapestries. Shown here (from New Place Museum) are a pair of tapestry panels, originally intended as cushion covers, which were woven at Barcheston towards the end of the six-teenth century. Both measure 21 by 18 in. and depict an allegorical scene which is continued from one panel into the next.

Gold sovereign of Elizabeth I (*obv.*)

Gold and silver coins of James I

Gold Rose Ryal of 30*s.* piece of James I (*rev.*)

16th-century Venetian silver ducat

Gold Rose Ryal of James I (*obv.*)

Gold and silver coins of Elizabeth I

Gold sovereign of Elizabeth I (*rev.*)

FURNITURE

The illustrations which follow give an impression of the range of the period furniture in the Trust's collection. The massive oak 'cupboard of boxes' (*below*) with its twelve drawers, double doors and three different locks, was made for the Corporation of Stratford in 1595.

An extending refectory table with carved supports, *c.* 1600 in date. The top is of a single plank of wood

Below: chests and coffers of various sizes and styles, each with carving displaying the skill and taste of the individual craftsman

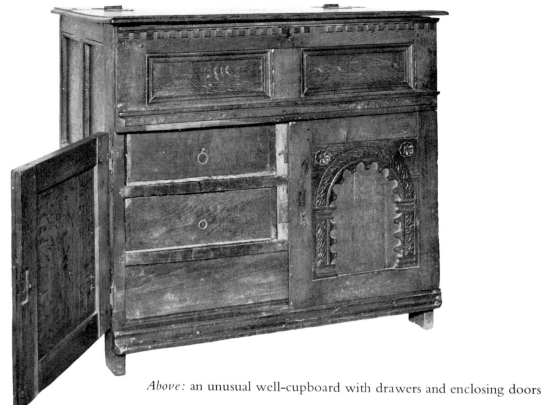

Above: an unusual well-cupboard with drawers and enclosing doors

Below: a clothes press (*left*) and court cupboard

Armchairs in variety, with a seat-table

FARMING AND RURAL LIFE

Besides horse-drawn implements, manual push or breast-ploughs were in common use for skimming light soils and cutting turf. The labourer pushing the plough wore a 'protector' as shown to protect his thighs.

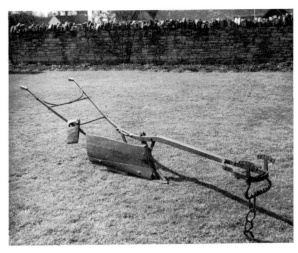

Above: two local types of horse-drawn ploughs, one with a single and the other with a double share. Ploughs similar to these were in use until the early years of the present century

Below: an early horse-drawn seed drill of simple mechanism. Although seed drills first appeared in England in the seventeenth century the broadcast sowing of seed by hand was still common until the last century

Sickles and fagging-hook

A wooden costrel

Root choppers

Early type of box chaff-cutter

Above: wheelwright's tools with wheel-turned lathe

Below left: thatching tools

Below right: moulds for brick making

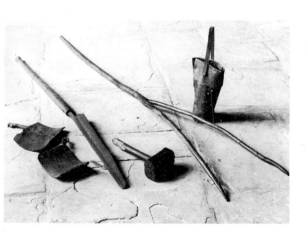

SHAKESPEARE COMMEMORATIVE MEDALS

Although there have been many Shakespeare medals in the past, no individual sculptor medallist had so far undertaken the task of producing a comprehensive series of medals depicting episodes and characters from each of Shakespeare's plays. In 1971 Paul Vincze, the eminent medallist who designed the official Shakespeare Anniversary medal in 1964, began work on a series of Shakespeare Commemorative Medals under the sponsorship of the Shakespeare Birthplace Trust which, when completed, will undoubtedly be recognised as one of the outstanding artistic achievements of the 1970's. Eight medals have been designed so far.

The obverse of each medal bears this new representation of Shakespeare set against a background of the Elizabethan stage

SBN 85306 403 2
© 1972 Jarrold & Sons Ltd, Norwich
Printed and published in Great Britain by Jarrold & Sons Ltd, Norwich 1972

THE
SHAKESPEARE BIRTHPLACE TRUST
1971–1981

AN EPILOGUE TO

In Honour of

SHAKESPEARE

by

LEVI FOX
Director of the Trust

PUBLISHED BY JARROLD AND SONS LIMITED, NORWICH
IN ASSOCIATION WITH
THE SHAKESPEARE BIRTHPLACE TRUST
STRATFORD-UPON-AVON
1982

INTRODUCTION

The decade 1971–81 has been a period of unprecedented development in the history of the Birthplace Trust.

The continued growth in the international appreciation of Shakespeare has brought greater numbers of visitors to Stratford-upon-Avon and the Shakespearian properties and, while this has increased the Trust's income, it has made necessary the provision of amenities and improved facilities and added to the responsibility and cost of maintaining the properties and their gardens. At the same time the development of the Trust's educational and academic activities has rendered necessary the building of an extension to the Shakespeare Centre, thus completing the original concept of a well-equipped headquarters for Shakespearian study and research. In its various departments the Trust now employs a staff of about 150.

Significant additions have been made to the Trust's collections. There has been a marked increase in the number of readers using the library and records office, with considerably greater demand for the Centre's facilities by visiting college groups and secondary schools. The established policy of presenting exhibitions has made more widely known the rich variety of material in the collections and on occasion special items have been loaned for display in this country and abroad.

Apart from its involvement with tourists and students the Trust has undertaken a number of major improvement schemes to the let properties it owns and made important contributions to the cause of conservation. Shops and houses in Henley Street have been bought to safeguard the environment of the Birthplace and at Shottery the bequest of Burnside, with its land and picturesque cottages (*see page 133, bottom left*), has made possible an extended conservation area around the Cottage. Shakespeare's parkland at Welcombe, also owned by the Trust, has now become a golf-course.

In discharge of its responsibilities in the wider sphere, the Trust has been instrumental in bringing into existence an organisation for linking together individuals and institutions interested in Shakespeare in every part of the

world. This is the International Shakespeare Association which has its headquarters at the Shakespeare Centre. The International Shakespeare Association's first congress, held in Washington, DC in 1976, was commemorated by a medal (*above*) struck by Paul Vincze; and a second congress held in Stratford-upon-Avon in 1981 attracted 660 delegates from thirty countries. The Trust has also continued to play a leading part in organising the annual Shakespeare Birthday Celebrations (*below*).

THE SHAKESPEARIAN PROPERTIES

As already indicated, the primary responsibility of the Trust is to preserve the Shakespearian properties as national memorials to the poet and to present them in a manner calculated to foster knowledge and appreciation of Shakespeare's life, work and time. It follows that a regular round of inspection and maintenance of the physical fabric of these historic buildings and their contents has to be undertaken, and the gardens which form an integral part of their attraction have to be kept up to a high standard. The Trust now has a considerable garden department with its own greenhouses and reserve gardens for growing flowers and its own team of craftsmen experienced in traditional skills who undertake the day-to-day maintenance of the properties.

Modern fire-detection and security devices have been installed in all the properties. During 1971–72 a major overhaul of the fabric of Shakespeare's Birthplace was undertaken. This involved attention to the Wilmcote stone foundation walls and chimney-stacks and the repair and treatment of the exterior timber framing. A portion of one of the original wattle and daub panels on the front of the house was exposed to view and protected and the fragile old window of the birthroom bearing the signatures of early visitors was encased on both sides.

A more difficult problem had to be dealt with at Mary Arden's House, caused by an attack of death-watch beetle following an exceptionally dry summer. During 1975–77 major remedial preservative treatment and renewal of certain

affected parts of the timber framing of the house nearest to the dovecote was undertaken.

Meanwhile important steps have been taken to safeguard the rural environment of Mary Arden's House. The Trustees have acquired the field opposite, together with Albany House with its large garden facing Station Road and the former Congregational chapel in Aston Cantlow Road with the object of preventing undesirable development. The Glebe Farm, situated immediately alongside Mary Arden's, has also been purchased with the object of conservation and with the long-term intention of linking the two farmsteads together to make possible an extended Shakespeare countryside museum. As a contribution towards providing more storage and display space for the growing farming and folk collection (*page 134 bottom right*) additional open-fronted hovels have been built in the rick-yard at Mary Arden's.

General repairs to Hall's Croft, including the rebuilding of the central chimney-stacks, have been undertaken and a complete spit mechanism installed in the kitchen there (*page 134 middle left*). The rear portion of Nash's House, previously occupied as caretaker's quarters, has been adapted to provide a period kitchen (*page 134*

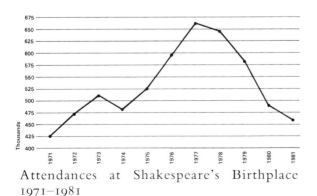

Attendances at Shakespeare's Birthplace
1971–1981

Top: Sundial in the Birthplace garden designed by John Skelton

THE SHAKESPEARIAN PROPERTIES

bottom left) and an upstairs gallery for the display of local history material (*page 134 top*).

The fact that the Shakespearian properties have become one of Britain's major tourist attractions has also brought problems of handling large numbers of visitors and providing for them modern amenities not normally found in period houses. In 1964, when all previous records were broken, the total number of visitors to the Shakespearian properties was 705,867, the number for Shakespeare's Birthplace alone being 321,760. By 1972 the Birthplace attracted 467,808 with a total of 1,065,132 for all the properties. Since then the annual total (*see graph on page 132*) has continued to exceed a million and during the Queen's Silver Jubilee year of 1977 peak attendances of 661,429 for the Birthplace and 1,486,210 for all the properties were reached.

New arrangements for the reception of visitors have been provided. A coach terminal (*page 132*) in Windsor Street handles all the coaches bringing visitors to the Birthplace. This together with a multi-storey car park (presented by the Trust to the town), was completed in February 1980 and a Visitors' Centre opened in 1981. Coach and car parks serving the Cottage have been extended and an amenity building (*page 133 top*) provided. To mark the Queen's Silver Jubilee the Trustees constructed a field path approach to the Cottage, known as Jubilee Walk (*page 133 bottom right*) from the centre of Shottery. A reception building and car park have also been added at Mary Arden's House (*page 134 middle right*).

Many distinguished personages have visited the properties during these years. During the Royal Shakespeare Theatre's centenary celebrations Her Majesty Queen Elizabeth II visited Hall's Croft on 27 June 1975 (*below*) and H.R.H. The Princess Anne, Mrs Mark Phillips, visited Shakespeare's Birthplace, the Shakespeare Centre and Anne Hathaway's Cottage on 27 May 1979 (*page 133 middle right*).

THE SHAKESPEARE CENTRE EXTENSION

When the original Centre was built its plan envisaged a possible extension at a future date to provide additional accommodation and facilities for the Trust's developing educational work. In the event the Centre proved so satisfactory in use that plans for an extension were considered by the Trustees in 1972. Several proposals failed to secure planning approval but a modified scheme evolved during 1977 was eventually agreed.

The architect of the Centre, Laurence Williams, designed the extension to a brief prepared by the Trust's Director, Dr Levi Fox. Construction began in January 1979 and the building was completed (*opposite top left*) in two years. It was officially opened by H.R.H. The Duchess of Kent on 25 June 1981.

The extension is an unusual complex comprising a number of different units each designed and equipped to discharge a particular function. Hidden away underneath is a spacious basement area comprising specially constructed storage rooms for the safe keeping of the Trust's library and archive collections and a new records office, approached from Guild Street, has been added.

Most of the ground floor is taken up with a reception foyer designed to serve as a Visitors' Centre (*opposite top right*) providing amenities for those visiting Shakespeare's Birthplace, the approach to which is now through the garden (*opposite bottom left*).

On the first and second floors is an assembly suite comprising rooms of varying sizes, ranging from the Queen Elizabeth Hall (*opposite bottom right*), with a seating capacity of 250 and the Wolfson Hall (*opposite right*) which can accommodate 100, to a series of smaller rooms suitable for seminar or meeting purposes. Amenities have not been forgotten, a bar being provided on the first floor and refreshment facilities for the King James I Lounge on the second floor. This type of accommodation represents something entirely new, both for the Trust and the town.

The extension building is also attractive by reason of its dignified décor and aesthetic quality. As with the original Centre, liberal use is made of traditional materials and the skills of living artists have been invoked to contribute a number of special embellishments associated with the concept and role of the building. In the Visitors' Centre a revolving skeletal model of a world globe (*opposite*) symbolises the universality of Shakespeare's appeal and a mural of ceramic tiles illustrates the rural character of Shakespeare's Stratford.

Plaque under the entrance portico of the Centre extension

Official opening ceremony performed by H.R.H. The Duchess of Kent

The collections already described are maintained and added to with the object of providing the best possible working reference resources for students and scholars engaged on research into the many aspects of Shakespearian subject-matter.

Bookbinding, repairs to records and conservation of archaeological artefacts and other items in the museum category are regularly undertaken as necessary, while the preparation of card index catalogues, finding lists and other reference aids continues all the time.

The library reading room provided in the original building (*see page 15*) has been supplemented with a seminar room (the Richard Field room) in the extension, together with audio-visual facilities for the development of the use of recorded and visual sources. The new records department has its own reading room (*below*) for readers wishing to consult the manuscript

collections, linked with an open access local history library and a seminar room (the Drayton room) for project work.

Each year copies of significant new publications on every aspect of Shakespearian subject-matter are acquired, together with relevant periodicals. Opportunity is also taken to fill gaps in the reference categories. The high cost of sixteenth- and seventeenth-century books limits the acquisition of early printed material but some rare items have been purchased.

Further titles have been added to the collection of publications of The Shakespeare Head Press, originally established and operated in Stratford-upon-Avon, and an interesting collection of books and papers belonging to the late Alan Dent, the theatre critic and writer, has been presented. Recorded material worthy of special mention includes a video cassette of the B.B.C.'s television film of the 1979 Shakespeare Birthday Celebrations and the National Geographic Society's documentary film, *Shakespeare of Stratford and London*.

Apart from the increased foreign content of the library (*see page 146*), the widening range of productions staged by the Royal Shakespeare Company in Stratford and London, or on tour, has led to a steady increase in the amount of theatre archive material deposited at the Centre. This unique collection of prompt books, photographs, designs, programmes and related documentation is in constant demand by researchers into theatre and stage history.

The last ten years have seen an unprecedented growth in the rate of accessions in the records department. Since 1971, over 270 separate accessions have been received compared with less than 240 over the previous twenty-seven years. Some of these consist of only one or two items, but others are very considerable in bulk. The material includes records of local businesses, clubs and societies, ephemera, photographs, property documents, maps and personal papers. Since the designation of the Trust in 1978 as the Diocesan Records Office for Stratford-upon-Avon and Shottery, local parish registers have been deposited, alongside the records of the local Nonconformist churches.

Apart from archaeological and folk material (*see pages 156–7*), museum accessions range from pestles and mortars (*below*), added to the growing collection of medical exhibits at Hall's Croft, to a yeoman's stickback chair (*right*) illustrative of rural craft, and two types of gypsy caravans (*above*) made by the Romany craftsman, Bill Wright, and restored by Jim Berry.

The inscription 'Liber R. Grace: ex dono amice D. Susanne Hall' identifies this book as having been given by Susanna Hall, Shakespeare's daughter, to Colonel Richard Grace, probably when Queen Henrietta Maria stayed at New Place in 1643. William Covell's *Polimenteia*, 1595 (*opposite*), contains a side-note reference to 'Sweet Shakspeare', one of the earliest in print.

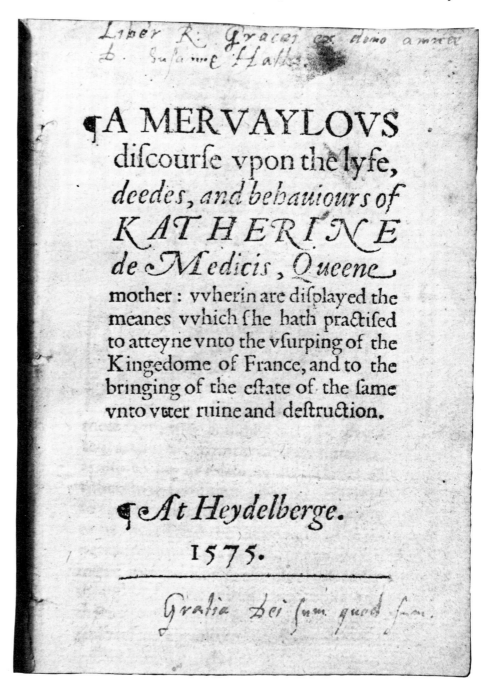

deard wit decking admired daughters)
write and let the worlde know that hea-
uens harmonie is no muficke, in refpect
of your fweete, and well arte-tuned
ftrings: that *Italian Ariofto* did but fha-
dowe the meaneft part of thy mufe, that
Taffos Godfrey is not worthie to make
compare with your truelie eternizing
Elizas ftile: let France-admired *Bellaw*,
and courtlike amarous *Roufard* con-
feffe that there be of your children, that
in thefe latter times haue farre furpaf-
fed them. Let diuine *Bartaffe* eternally
praife worthie for his weeks worke, fay
the beft thinges were made firft: Let o-
ther countries (fweet *Cambridge*) enuie,
(yet admire) my *Virgil*, thy petrarch, diuine *Spenfer*. And vnleffe I erre, (a thing
eafie in fuch fimplicitie) deluded by
dearlie beloued *Delia*, and fortunatelie
fortunate *Cleopatra*; *Oxford* thou maift
extoll thy courte-deare-verfe happie
Daniell, whofe fweete refined mufe, in
contracted fhape, were fufficient a-
mongft

Marginal notes:
M. Alabla-fter. Spenfer and others.

Lylia clou-ded, whofe teares are making.

All praife worthy. Lucrecia Sweet Shak-fpeare. Eloquent Gaueston.

BOOKS OF SHAKESPEARE'S PERIOD

It is not always appreciated that the Elizabethan Age saw the publication of books on almost every conceivable type of subject-matter. Some of them provided source material for Shakespeare's plays *(see page 46)*.

Among books on sports and pastimes George Turbeville's *The noble art of venerie or hunting* and *The booke of falconrie or hauking*, both published in 1575, became standard reference works. As shown on this page their woodcut illustrations are particularly attractive.

A good number of classical texts were available in English translations. One of these was Arthur Goldinge's version of Caesar's Gallic Wars (1565) shown opposite.

Education was also well represented by various textbooks and manuals of instruction. John Withal's *Dictionarie* for children was first published in 1563 and later augmented with verses, as shown in the 1608 edition illustrated opposite.

oꝛ Prince, Curia, æ, fœ gen.

Si curiam curas, pariet tibi curia curas, If for the court thou takest care, the court will breed thee thought and care.

The corruption of the iudgment place, Tabes fori.

No truth is left in iudges, De foro sublata fides.

Men of one company or ward, Curiales.

A Parliament house, Senaculum.

Counsell, aduise, Consilium, lij, neut. gen.

Consilii flore pollens hic viuit honore, That man in honour doth liue and excell.

That passeth in wisedome and giuing counsell.

To aske counsell, Consulo, lis, lui, tum, cum Accusatiuo

Counselling, the particip. Consulens, tis, The impersonall verbe is Consulitur, that is, euery man sheweth his opinion, aduise. The passiue verbe is Consulor, eris, which is, to be counselled with, or sought vnto for counsel, aduise. And the aduerb Consulte, and Consultò, that is aduisedly wisely, discreetly.

He, and thee, that giueth, or asketh counsell,

Consultor, oris, m. g. Consultrix, icis, f.g.

That is consulted vpon, Consultum, ti, n.g.

—priùs ipsam consule mens, Quam vox exiliat, est irrevocabile verbum, First aske thou aduise and counsell of wit. Before thy tongue tattle, for if a word stir, recalling back serueth no reasking of it.

But Consulo with a Datiue case, is to giue counsell.

To command, Impero, as, & imperito, tas.

The seate where the iudge sitteth, Tribunal, lis, pinei, vel subsellium prætoris.

Before the iudgement seat, Pro tribunali.

A counsell-house, Concilibulum, li.

The worthie companie of learned men, Nobile concilium doctorum.

The place where Maisteries and Plaies be shewed.

A Theater, Theatrum, tri, n. gen.

Of, or belonging to a Theater, Theatralis, & hoc Theatricus, a, um, art

and theatridium, dij, n.g. is the diminutiue. A little Theater, Play house.

A maker, or wiser inuentor of Tragedies, Tragographus, i, and Tragicus, ci, m.g.

A tragicall Comedie, that is a Comedie in part, a Tragedie in part, mixed with mirth & mourning, Tragicomœdia, æ, f.g.

—vita hæc est fabula quædã, Scena autem mundus, versatilis histrio, & actor quilibet est hominum. This life is a certayne Enterlude or play, The world is a Stage full of change euery way, Euery man is a Player, and therein a dealer.

—spissis indigna theatris Scripta pudet recitare, & nugis ad.lere pondus, I am ashamed to rehearse their writings vnworthy of ful theaters, that is, great audience of people, and to make their toyes weightie.

A Player, Actor, toris, vel ludio, onis.

That acteth, or that playeth in a tragedie, Tragœdus, di, m.g.

Tragically, cruelly, Tragicé, aduerb.

A Tennis play, Sphæristerium.

Hee that beholdeth or looketh vppon the players, Spectator, toris.

A Sword player, Gladiator, toris.

Ecce Theatralem ingressus gladiator arenam, Lo, behold the Sword player is entred the Theater to play his Prize.

Halfe a Theater, also Heauen, Amphitheatrum, amphitheatri, n.g.

Omnipotens ille astriferi faber amphitheatri, That same almightie maker of the starrie halfe Theater, that is, the heauen and ye Skie.

The art of fighting with a Sword, Gladiatura.

A Maister of fence, Lanista, m.g.

To defend, preserue, keep from, Defendo, dis, di, the Passiue is Defendor, eris, to be defended

That defence, Defensatio, and Defensio, onis, f.g.

That is defended, preserued, &c. Defensus, a, um.

Certamen suum egit summa cum laude lanista, The Fence-maister hath played his Prize with great praise.

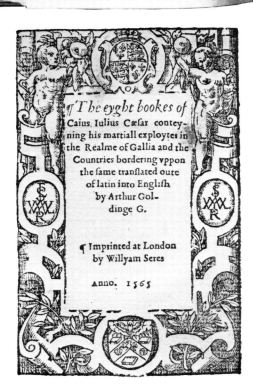

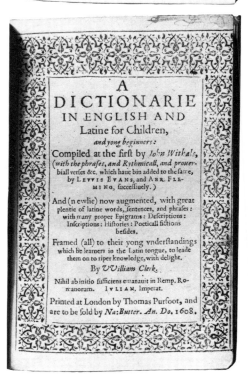

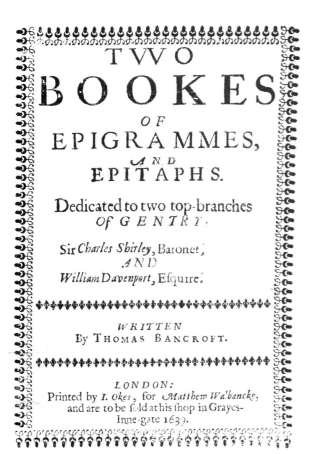

TVVO
BOOKES
OF
EPIGRAMMES,
AND
EPITAPHS.

Dedicated to two top-branches
Of GENTRY.

Sir *Charles Shirley*, Baronet,
AND
William Davenport, Esquire.

✦✦✦✦✦✦✦✦✦✦✦✦✦✦✦✦✦✦✦✦✦✦

WRITTEN
By THOMAS BANCROFT.

✦✦✦✦✦✦✦✦✦✦✦✦✦✦✦✦✦✦✦✦✦✦

LONDON:
Printed by *I. Okes*, for *Matthew Walbancke*,
and are to be sold at his shop in Grayes-
Inne-gate 1639.

Thomas Bancroft's volume (1639) contains two epigrams on Shakespeare, acknowledging his pre-eminence as a dramatist.

Niccolò Macchiavelli's *The Arte of Warre*, 1588

The Anatomie
of Abuses:

Containing

A Discouerie, or briefe Sum-
marie of such Notable Vices and Corrupti-
ons, as nowe raigne in many Christian Coun-
treyes of the Worlde : but (especially) in the
Countrey of AILGNA: Together, with most
fearefull Examples of Gods Iudgementes, ex-
ecuted vpon the wicked for the same, aswell in AILGNA of late, as in
other places, else-
where.

Very godly, to be read of all true Chri-
stians, euery where: but most chiefly, to be
regarded in England.

Made Dialogue-wise by PHILLIP STVBS.
And now newly reuised recognized, and aug-
mented the third time by the same Author.

MATH.3.ver.2.
Repent, for the kingdome of God is at hande.
LVKE.13.ver.5.
I say vnto you, except you repent you shall all perish.

Printed at London, **by** Richard
Iones 1 5 8 5.

Philip Stubbes's *The Anatomie of Abuses*, augmented edition 1585

Ch. R., *An Olde Thrift newly revived*, 1612

AN OLDE
THRIFT NEWLY
REVIVED.
WHEREIN IS DECLA-
RED THE MANNER OF
PLANTING, PRESERVING, AND
Husbanding yong Trees of diuers kindes for
Timber and Fuell.
AND OF SOWING ACORNES,
CHESNVTS, BEECH-MAST, THE SEEDES OF
Elmes, Athen-keyes, &c. With the Commodities
and Discommodities of Inclosing decayed
Forrests, Commons, and waste
GROVNDS.

And also the vse of a small portable Instrument for measuring of Board, and the solid content and height
of any Tree standing.

Discoursed in Dialogue betweene a Surueyour, Woodward,
Gentleman, and a Farmer.

Diuided into foure parts, by *R. C.*

Tout pour L'Eglise.

LONDON,
Printed by *W. S.* for *Richard Moore*, and are to be sold
at his shop in St. Dunstanes Churchyard,
1 6 1 2.

FINE PRINTING

Shakespeare's plays and poems have inspired many finely printed editions, such as The Shakespeare Head Press *Venus and Adonis*, 1909; the Doves Press *Hamlet*, 1909; The Shakespeare Head Press illustrated *Shepheardes Calendar*, 1930; and the Royal Shakespeare Theatre edition of the *Sonnets*, 1975.

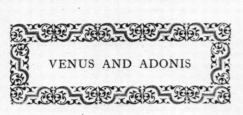

E VEN as the sun with purple-colour'd face
   Had ta'en his last leave of the weeping morn,
Rose-cheekt Adonis hied him to the chase;
Hunting he loved, but love he laught to scorn:
  Sick-thoughted Venus makes amain unto him,
  And like a bold-faced suitor 'gins to woo him.

"Thrice-fairer than myself," thus she began,
"The field's chief flower, sweet above compare,
Stain to all nymphs, more lovely than a man,
More white and red than doves or roses are;   10
  Nature that made thee, with herself at strife,
  Saith that the world hath ending with thy life.

"Vouchsafe, thou wonder, to alight thy steed,
And rein his proud head to the saddle-bow;
If thou wilt deign this favour, for thy meed
A thousand honey secrets shalt thou know:
  Here come and sit, where never serpent hisses,
  And being set, I'll smother thee with kisses;

                                       B

Thou blinde foole love, what doost thou to mine eyes,
That they behold and see not what they see:
They know what beautie is, see where it lyes,
Yet what the best is, take the worst to be.
If eyes corrupt by over-partiall lookes,
Be anchord in the baye where all men ride,
Why of eyes falsehood hast thou forged hookes,
Whereto the judgement of my heart is tide?
Why should my heart thinke that a severall plot,
Which my heart knowes the wide worlds common place?
Or mine eyes seeing this, say this is not
To put faire truth upon so foule a face,
  In things right true my heart and eyes have erred,
  And to this false plague are they now transferred.

ENTER BARNARDO, AND FRANCISCO,
TWO CENTINELS.

Bar. W HOSE THERE?
Fran.   Nay answere me. Stand & vnfolde your selfe.
Bar. Long liue the King.
Fran. Barnardo.
Bar. Hee.
Fran. You come most carefully vpon your houre.
Bar. Tis now strooke twelfe, get thee to bed Francisco.
Fran. For this reliefe much thanks, tis bitter cold,
And I am sick at hart.
Bar. Haue you had quiet guard?
Fran. Not a mouse stirring.
Bar. Well, good night:
If you doe meete Horatio and Marcellus,
The riualls of my watch, bid them make hast.

    Enter Horatio, and Marcellus.

Fran. I thinke I heare them, stand ho, who is there?
Hora. Friends to this ground.
Mar. And Leedgemen to the Dane.
Fran. Giue you good night.
Mar. O, farwell honest souldiers, who hath relieu'd you?
Fran. Barnardo hath my place; giue you good night.

    Exit Francisco.

Mar. Holla, Barnardo.
Bar. Say, what is Horatio there?

                      7

JANUARYE

ÆGLOGA·PRIMA
        ARGUMENT.
IN THIS FYRST ÆGLOGUE *Colin cloute* a shepheardes
boy complaineth him of his unfortunate love, being but
newly (as semeth) enamoured of a countrie lasse called
Rosalinde: with which strong affection being very sore
traveled, he compareth his carefull case to the sadde
season of the yeare, to the frostie ground, to the fro-
sen trees, and to his owne winterbeaten flocke.
  And lastlye, fynding himselfe robbed of all
former pleasaunce and delights, hee
breaketh his Pipe in peeces,
and casteth him selfe
to the ground.
    10

145

TRANSLATIONS AND
RECORDED SOURCES

Hardly a year passes without the publication of new translations of Shakespeare's plays or sonnets. The Centre library has translations into upwards of seventy languages. Some are illustrated and, as suggested by this selection (*right*), bear very attractive cover or dust-wrapper designs.

Another rapidly expanding category of library holdings comprises records, tapes, cassettes and video recordings of productions. Commentaries and readings from the plays and sonnets are also represented.

THEATRICAL MATERIAL

Included in the Centre's extensive collection of theatrical material are prompt books, costume designs and production records. Leslie Hurry's designs for *Troilus and Cressida*, 1960 and *Romeo* from a Royal Shakespeare Theatre poster (*above*); J. P. Kemble's Covent Garden prompt copy of *Henry V* (*below*).

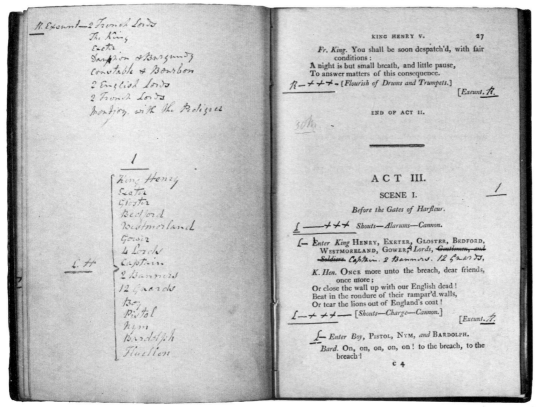

SHAKESPEARE IN ART

The series of Shake-
speare illustrations
by the artist and
caricaturist, Henry
William Bunbury
(1750–1811) en-
joyed considerable
popularity when re-
produced as hand-
coloured engraved
plates. They are par-
ticularly valuable as
a record of the
Georgian theatre.

These two origi-
nal drawings depict
Romeo and Juliet
in Friar Laurence's
cell (*above*) and the
supposed death
of Imogen in
Cymbeline.

SHAKESPEARIANA

Shakespeare memorabilia in variety. Below is a Chippendale garden chair which belonged to David Garrick. The name-plaque (*right centre*) came from HM submarine *Shakespeare*.

SHAKESPEARIAN MEDALLIONS

The Trust's collection includes representative Shakespeare medals struck from the time of the Garrick Jubilee of 1769 onwards. Its most recent addition is the unique series of thirty-six medallions (the original bronzes are displayed in the Birthplace Visitors' Centre) portraying scenes and characters from Shakespeare's plays designed by the medallic sculptor, Paul Vincze, whose work is well known throughout the world. Vincze designed the official 1964 Shakespeare anniversary medal (*see page 36*), the medal commemorating the 200th anniversary of the Garrick Jubilee and the medal struck to mark the first Congress of the International Shakespeare Association (*see page 131*).

The illustrations opposite demonstrate the individual quality and appeal of Paul Vincze's medals. Each subject exemplifies the technical skill of an artist who has a complete mastery of the medallic medium. Invariably his compositions are well balanced and his characters portrayed with sympathy and lifelike reality.

LOCAL BUSINESS RECORDS

Stratford's prosperity during the past 150 years is attributable to two main factors: the growing appreciation of Shakespeare and the increasing popularity of the town as a place of international pilgrimage; and the development of a number of varied light industries, trades and business enterprises.

Local business records accordingly constitute important historical source material and as such the Trust has provided facilities for their safe keeping. The records of Flowers Brewery, founded in 1831 and pictured below in a sketch as it was in 1870, form a major deposit.

STRATFORD EPHEMERA

As illustrated by these examples, a single poster, handbill, advertisement or programme can illuminate an event or little-known aspect of local history. The Trust continues to add to its considerable collection of material of this kind and the subject-matter covered is so miscellaneous as to make classification difficult.

In 1863 Stratford celebrated a royal marriage in grand style (*below*). Special measures were taken to relieve distress caused by local unemployment in 1888 (*right*). Meanwhile, the proposed new church (St James's in Guild Street, now demolished) was built in 1853–54.

To the Worshipful the Mayor of Stratford-on-Avon.

We, the undersigned Burgesses of Stratford-on-Avon, considering the amount of distress now existing in this Borough and its immediate Neighbourhood owing to the scarcity of Work, request your Worship to call a

PUBLIC MEETING

To consider the advisability of Opening a

SOUP KITCHEN.

ROB. GIBBS.	RICH. HAWKES.
W. G. COLBOURNE.	CHAS. GIBBS.
R. M. BIRD.	J. FARMER.
H. W. NEWTON.	FRED WINTER.
JAS. COX.	W. E. EAVES.
JOHN MORGAN.	JOHN PARKER.
J. J. KEMP.	THOMAS C. NEW.
ALFD. RIDER.	CHARLES WYE.
J. G. REYNOLDS.	THOS. J. OLNEY.
W. H. EATON.	ROBERT GUY.
W. S. HOYLES	C. THOMAS.
THOS. WOMACK.	D. DRINKWATER.
W. J. NORRIS.	H. SELLERS.
EDWARD FOX.	

I, the undersigned, in accordance with the above requisition, do hereby convene a MEETING of the INHABITANTS of the Town and Neighbourhood in the UPPER ROOM OF THE TOWN HALL, TO-MORROW, January 19th, 1888, at Three o'clock in the Afternoon.

ARTHUR HODGSON,
Mayor.

January 18th, 1888.

HERALD PRINTING WORKS, STRATFORD-ON-AVON.

V.   R.

MARRIAGE
OF THE
PRINCE OF WALES!!
March 10th, 1863.

STRATFORD-UPON-AVON
CELEBRATION.

GENERAL PROGRAMME:
6 a.m.—DISCHARGE OF ARTILLERY.
7 a.m.—Church Bells to Ring.
9 a.m.
RUSTIC SPORTS TO COMMENCE!
10.30 a.m.
GRAND DONKEY RACES!!
At Noon a Royal Salute of 21 guns.
1.0 P.M.—PROCESSION TO ASSEMBLE.
2 p.m.
THE PROCESSION TO COMMENCE PERAMBULATING THE TOWN.
ROUTE:—
From Rother Street to Bree Street, Church Street, Chapel Street, High Street, Wood Street, Windsor Street, Henley Street, Union Street, Guild Street, Bridge Street.
3 p.m.—DISCHARGE OF ARTILLERY.
4 p.m.
The Procession to be Massed in Bridge-street & the "NATIONAL ANTHEM" sung.
School Children to be Regaled.
5 p.m.
BANQUET AT THE RED HORSE HOTEL.
6 p.m.—DISCHARGE OF ARTILLERY.
8 p.m.
THE ILLUMINATIONS TO BE LIGHTED.
9 p.m.
GRAND DISPLAY OF FIREWORKS!!
AT THE MARKET CROSS.
10 p.m.
BALL AT THE TOWN HALL!

The Committee express their earnest hope that all Persons will afford protection to the School Children in the Procession, and wear Wedding Favors of White Coventry Ribbon; and they invite their Fellow-Townsmen to aid the general effect by displaying Flags and Evergreens.
The Public are requested not to crowd the Procession or follow it, but to keep their places on the Pavement as far as practicable; and it is desired that Vehicles may during the afternoon be kept out of the Streets through which the Procession will pass.

By order of the Committee,
JOHN MORGAN, } Secretaries.
R. LAPWORTH,

E. ADAMS, PRINTER, "HERALD" OFFICE, STRATFORD-ON-AVON.

PROPOSED
NEW CHURCH
AT
STRATFORD-ON-AVON.

PUBLIC MEETING.

We, the undersigned, invite the Inhabitants of Stratford-on-Avon and the neighbourhood, to meet us in the TOWN HALL, (the use of which has been kindly granted for the occasion by the Worshipful the MAYOR,) on WEDNESDAY NEXT, December 10, at Eleven o'clock in the forenoon, for the purpose of taking into consideration the expediency of erecting a Church at, or in the immediate neighbourhood of New Town, Stratford-on-Avon.

HENRY HARDING, M.A., VICAR
THOMAS MASON
E. D. FORD
FISHER TOMES
T. R. MEDWIN, M.A.
JOHN HARDY
DAVID RICE
HENRY TWELLS, M.A.
F. FORTESCUE KNOTTESFORD, M.A.
W. O. HUNT
W. SHELDON
THOMAS D. GILL
R. CHATTAWAY
JOHN GARDNER
JOHN GILL

Stratford-on-Avon,
Dec. 5, 1851.

F. & E. WARD, PRINTERS, BOOKSELLERS, AND STATIONERS, STRATFORD-UPON-AVON.

Records illustrating the restoration of Shakespeare's Birthplace 1861–62 (*above*). Early school attendance register (*below*).

LOCAL VIEWS

Stratford has been well recorded by artists and photographers, probably due to its Shakespearian associations. It is therefore possible, with the help of the Trust's topographical collection, to re-create street scenes at different periods and to illustrate the physical change of particular buildings. Examples are High Street before the coming of the motor car (*right*), Bridge Street with its open street market (*below*), and a panoramic view of the town in 1864.

STRATFORD-ON-AVON 1864

ARCHAEOLOGICAL MATERIAL

Substantial additions of important archaeological material illustrative of the Roman and Anglo-Saxon periods of settlement in Stratford have been made as a result of further excavations on sites in the river valley alongside the Tiddington road. The finds include pottery, coins, miscellaneous domestic items (*right*), brooches (*below*), beads and other jewellery worn by women together with the remains of spears, knives and shields used by the menfolk (*bottom*).

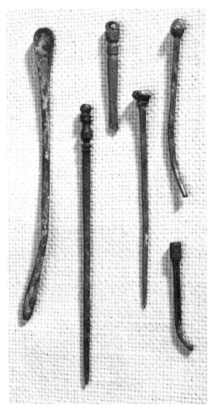

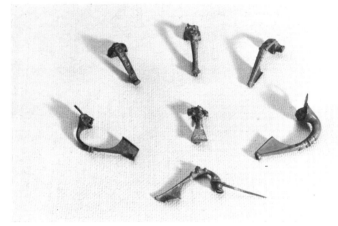

FOLK COLLECTION

Examples of almost every kind of item illustrating different aspects of rural life continue to be added to the Shakespeare countryside museum at Mary Arden's House. Here are shown a cider-press (*below*); a portable blacksmith's forge and tools (*right*); an odometer for measuring distances (*below right*); instruments from the Langley village band (*below centre*); and a mantrap and a warning notice for deterring poachers (*below left*).

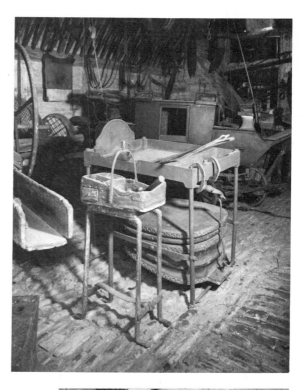

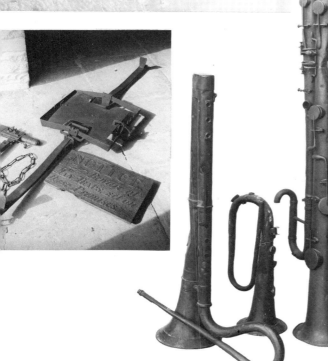

IN HONOUR OF SHAKESPEARE

Speech delivered by Dr Louis B. Wright on the occasion of a party held at the Shakespeare Centre to commemorate the 125th anniversary of the purchase of Shakespeare's Birthplace for preservation as a national memorial 16 September 1972

Mr Flower, Dr Fox, My Lords, My Lord Bishop, Distinguished Guests,

First let me express my deep appreciation to the Director and Trustees for inviting me to come as a special guest on this occasion. For more than 125 years my countrymen have been attracted to Stratford. During the Middle Ages men and women thought they had to make a pilgrimage to Santiago de Compostela for the salvation of their souls. In later times millions of Americans, with almost the devotion of medieval pilgrims, have come to Stratford for their cultural salvation. They have even bought bushels of holy relics to take back to the United States. One great collector, Henry Clay Folger, acquired enough of Shakespeare's mulberry tree to make a fair reconstruction of that miraculous growth. When I became Director of the Folger Shakespeare Library I discovered in the attic a bundle of sticks carefully tied up in red tape and labelled: 'Splinters from a pew in Holy Trinity Church'. These had been bought at a price from an American dealer. How much kindling wood has been thus translated into pure gold I do not know.

For more than forty years I, too, have been a pilgrim constantly returning to Stratford. It is a matter of satisfaction to see the enormous improvement in that time in the way Shakespeare has been made vivid and significant to the throngs who regard Stratford as their Mecca. The present Director and his staff have worked wonders in recent years and deserve the world's gratitude. They have made a visit to Stratford an occasion of both delight and instruction.

Dr Fox, the distinguished administrator of the Birthplace Trust, has a great reputation on both sides of the Atlantic, and I would like at this point to express my admiration for the phenomenal accomplishments that have taken place during his term of office. The combination of historical learning and extraordinary administrative ability in the same personality is rare. The Birthplace Trust has been fortunate in finding such a personality as Dr Fox. The wise policy of property acquisition in recent years has done much to preserve the ancient heritage of Stratford. Dr Fox has also been able to organise the physical assets of the Birthplace Trust into an institution of paramount importance for the cultural and intellectual benefit of the thousands who come to Stratford. Only those who have seen the transformation that has taken place in recent years can realise the full significance of this change. At this time, it is a pleasure for me to pay a tribute to Dr Fox for what he has done.

If legend is to be believed, Stratford owes a debt to an American who may not be remembered on this side of the Atlantic. He was Phineas T. Barnum, showman and circus magnate, who made an effort to buy the Birthplace in the period just before 1847. Barnum claimed that the threat of his carting off the Birthplace, stick and stone, to exhibit in his Museum in New York (along with his midgets, stuffed animals, a Fiji mermaid, and the 'very club that killed Captain Cook') stirred the British to buy the Birthplace and save it for the nation. That may be an apocryphal story; Barnum was not above drawing a long bow. But in his autobiography, *Barnum's Own Story*, he wrote:

> During my first visit to England I obtained verbally, through a friend, the refusal of the house in which Shakespeare was born, designing to remove it in sections to my Museum in New York; but the project leaked out, British pride was touched, and several English gentlemen interfered and purchased the premises for a Shakespearian Association. Had they slept a few days longer, I should have made a rare speculation, for I was subsequently assured that the British people, rather than suffer that house to be removed to America, would have bought me off with twenty thousand pounds.

For many reasons I am glad that America does not have to bear the onus of robbing Britain of this national treasure. We have enough sins to answer for as it is. But Barnum's instinct for what his countrymen would pay to see was correct. Any place even named Stratford can now set up in the theatrical business and do well. We have Shakespeare festivals at Stratford, Connecticut, and Stratford, Ontario, that attract visitors from the whole North American continent. Three weeks ago I visited Ashland, Oregon, a country town of 13,000 inhabitants in the north-west part of the United States. There for the past thirty-seven years a Shakespeare theatre has flourished without foundation support or subsidy of any kind. Ashland has also become a place of pilgrimage for thousands of Americans because it has played Shakespeare straight, without distracting gimmicks and without reading into his works meanings that the poet never intended. As a result Shakespeare has become Ashland's most lucrative industry.

Long before Barnum's realisation of the appeal of the Birthplace, Americans had been coming to Stratford, visiting the Birthplace – and buying relics. The best remembered of these early visitors was Washington Irving who first arrived in 1815. In his *Sketchbook*, published in 1820, he tells of his experience at the Birthplace. This of course may be an old story to Dr Fox and others but, at the risk of repeating a twice-told tale, let me quote a few lines:

> My first visit was to the house where Shakespeare was born. . . . It is a small mean-looking edifice of wood and plaster, a true nestling-place of genius, which seems to delight in hatching its off-spring in by-corners. The walls of its squalid chambers are covered with names and inscriptions in every language, by pilgrims of all nations, ranks, and conditions from the prince to the peasant, and present a simple but striking instance of the spontaneous and universal homage of mankind to the great poet of nature.

Let us hope that such 'spontaneous and universal homage' no longer moves the multitude to scribble on the walls. Dr Fox has problems enough without such 'homage'.

Irving continued his comment:

> The house is shown by a garrulous old lady in a frosty red face, lighted up by a cold blue anxious eye, and garnished with artificial locks of flaxen hair, curling from under an exceedingly dirty cap. She was particularly assiduous in exhibiting the relics with which this, like all other celebrated shrines, abounds. There was the shattered stock of the very match-lock with which Shakespeare shot the deer on his poaching exploits. There, too, was his tobacco box; . . . the sword also with

'*Sketch from the sale of Shakespeare's House, at the Auction Mart, Sept. 16, 1847.*'

which he played Hamlet; and the identical lantern with which Friar Laurence discovered Romeo and Juliet in the tomb. There was an ample supply also of Shakespeare's mulberry-tree, which seems to have had as extraordinary powers of self-multiplication as the wood of the true Cross, of which there is enough extant to build a ship of the line. The most favourite object of curiosity, however, is Shakespeare's chair.

In time, I regret to say, many of my countrymen acquired these relics. During my time at the Folger hardly a week passed that someone did not want to sell or even to give us some of these wonders. A worthy woman insisted upon presenting us with Shakespeare's walking-stick. Folger himself had long before acquired two such sticks, one said to have been 'cut from the crabtree' under which, according to legend, Shakespeare slept on his way home from a drinking bout with the boys at Bidford.

I mention this merely to show the tangible appeal of Shakespeare through the centuries. I was about to say 'touching' appeal, without meaning to pun. Anything that could be connected with the dramatist took on a special virtue. Few saints have ever had more pious believers and collectors of their relics.

Oddly enough, however, it took some time for Stratford to realise the treasure that it possessed. Even yet, I gather, there are those in the town who only dimly realise that Shakespeare is one of Britain's most profitable attractions for tourists who bring millions of pounds to this country each year. We in America are now vastly distressed about our unfavourable balance of payments, and pilgrims who come to visit Shakespeare's Warwickshire, and leave their money behind them, are among the villains that the Federal Reserve Bank would like to curb. Shakespeare has become an industry of national as well as local profit. In the unlikely event that Stratford could swap Shakespeare for an aluminium pie-plate factory, England, as well as Stratford, would be the financial loser. Never in history has a poet managed to create such a far-reaching industry.

Yet in 1805, when the Birthplace was advertised to be sold at auction, the broadside made no mention of its association with Shakespeare. The advertising broadside simply announced:

> To be Sold By Auction By T. Taylor, At The White-Lion Inn in Stratford-upon-Avon, On Thursday the 7th Day of March, 1805, Between The Hours of Three and Five In The Afternoon . . . Two Freehold Dwelling Houses, with the Stables, Outbuildings, and Yards belonging to the same, very eligibly situated in Henley Street in the Borough of Stratford-upon-Avon: one of which has been more than a Century and is now used as a Public-House, known by the Sign of the Swan and Maidenhead—The above Premises are in the several occupations of Joseph Jobson and William Hornsby [corrected in pen to read Thomas Hornby]. For further particulars apply to Mr. Wheler, Solicitor, Stratford-upon-Avon.

The story of the further vicissitudes of the Birthplace are not my concern at the moment, and will be better told by others, but I would like to mention a performance in London on 7 December 1847, at the Royal Italian Opera House in Covent Garden to raise money in aid of the fund to purchase the Birthplace. The best

actors and actresses joined in giving scenes from nine of Shakespeare's plays. Charles Knight, the editor and publisher, wrote a prologue spoken by Mr Phelps in which these lines occur:

> But Shakespeare's home, his boyhood's home is ours.
> Ye, who this night kind greetings bring to cheer
> The histrionic groups assembled here,—
> Cherish the task, with reverent love to hold
> One relic of our drama's age of gold.
>
> The Pilgrims come: Ohio and the Rhine
> Send forth their worshippers to Stratford's shrine,—
> And still they come to hail, from every clime,
> The Poet of all countries and 'all time'.
> Is the work finish'd—or but yet begun?
> Complete! Maintain! Do all that needs be done!
> Yes! England's heart now beats at Shakespeare's call
> The Muses' bower is saved—yours is the pledge for All.

The task of completing, preserving, and maintaining, pledged in 1847, still requires the kind of effort and vigilance that the present Director and Trustees so ably demonstrate. The task is endless but infinitely worth while. Meanwhile the pilgrims continue to come, not only from Ohio and the Rhine, but from all the world. And they now go away with something better than fake relics. Thanks to instructive exhibitions, carefully planned lectures and a variety of other educational offerings by the Birthplace Trust, the pilgrims return more learned and more inspired than when they came. That day in 1847 when the Shakespeare Association acquired the Birthplace was fortunate for Stratford and the world.

1983 Edition with additional 32pp: 0 7117 0044 3
© 1983 Jarrold & Sons Ltd, Norwich. Printed and published in Great Britain by Jarrold & Sons Ltd, Norwich 283